UP THE BEANSTALK AGAIN

Alan Marshall

Published by Playstage
United Kingdom.

An imprint of Write Publications Ltd

www.playsforadults.com

Designed by Kate Lowe, Greensands Graphics
Printed by Creeds Ltd, Bridport, Dorset

Note to producers about staging "Up The Beanstalk Again"

The action of the play is divided into two areas – the reality of the backstage dressing room and the unreality of the pantomime stage. This could be achieved by three methods:

a) dividing the stage into two areas so that one side of the stage is the panto area and the other side is the dressing room. Each side would be lit when action takes place and go dark when there is no action. If this method is used then it is recommended that you have some representational scenery in the panto area, to balance the aesthetics of the stage. For example, two flats painted to show a village scene or a woodland scene, as per pantomime style.

b) a more ambitious staging would be to have the scenery for the dressing room and the panto, back-to-back on a platform that could be revolved. However, the presence of stage hands to perform this action could detract from the dramatic content of the piece.

c) for a small stage, the simplest solution would be to have the dressing room scene centre stage, behind the proscenium, and all panto action to take place in front of the closed curtains. If this option is chosen, then the final scene where ANGELA and LAURENCE speak their monologues in tight spotlights would have to be done with the curtains open.

It is important to keep the pace up in many parts of this play. ANGELA and LAURENCE are constantly bickering when they are together and the panto scenes should be quick-fire. This allows the pace of the monologues and moments of tragedy to slacken for dramatic effect.

The characters: LAURENCE, although playing a camp part in the pantomime scenes, should not be camp throughout the play. He should have the presence and controlled power of a once-superb classical actor. ANGELA, while a fragile personality, is not submissive. She "gives as good as she gets" when in confrontation with LAURENCE. PAT and ERIC are sweet, old fashioned people. JACK is tough, ambitious, insensitive and self-obsessed. GEMMA is a nice girl from a theatrical family. She admires JACK but is sensible enough to see that he is not a very nice person.

CAST (In order of appearance)

ANGELA   A former actress, now wardrobe mistress and Laurence's companion/friend. In her sixties.

GEMMA   Assistant stage manager, aged nineteen.

LAURENCE   One time classical actor, now a pantomime dame. In his late sixties. Still handsome, with presence.

HARRY   Stage door keeper. Ordinary and unassuming man in his sixties.

'JACK'   TV soap star, in his early twenties.

PAT   Front end of Daisy the cow. In her late fifties.

ERIC   Pat's husband. The back end of Daisy the cow. He also doubles as Baron Soft Touch. Also in his late fifties.

PROMPT   (offstage voice – two lines)

Four male and three female parts plus offstage voice.

The action takes place in LAURENCE's dressing room and onstage for a pantomime in a regional theatre.

UP THE BEANSTALK AGAIN
ACT 1 SCENE 1

*The action takes place in a provincial theatre on Christmas Eve, in
LAURENCE BEDFORD'S dressing room. Any pantomime action takes
place in front of the stage – each change is created with lighting.*

*In the dressing room ANGELA is sewing a torn costume. The dressing room
contains a make up table and mirror, with lights, a couch, a fridge, a dress
rack on which hang all LAURENCE's extravagant costumes and, on the
wall facing the audience a large photo(or painting) of LAURENCE's
mother – an elegant, unsmiling, elderly woman in evening dress. It dominates
the whole room. There are various wigs on stands on the make-up table
plus jewellery and make-up. The wall is covered in Christmas cards and
there are one or two Christmas decorations up. There is a door in the wall
facing the audience.*

ANGELA   *(to herself, crossly)* I How many times do I have to sew this
bit up? Why don't we just buy the material and make a new
one? Because we're too bloody mean, that's why. *(Looking
up at the portrait)* Aren't we Gloria? We've had a lifetime of
handing over all our money to mummy and we never spend
anything on ourselves do we? Don't look at me like that
you old cow. I hope you're rotting in your grave... *(She
finishes her sewing, snaps off the thread and holds the frock
up against her)* There, Gloria, what do you think?
Absolutely ghastly – you're quite right, but then you don't
care what your son looks like, do you? Your wonderful,
talented son.....

GEMMA   *(sticking her head round the door)* Angela, he's coming off for the change!

ANGELA   *(springing to her feet and grabbing a frock off the rack)* Oh my God! It's gone quick today hasn't it?

GEMMA   That's cos Jack cut three pages out of the script. *(GEMMA stands to one side and waits for LAURENCE)*

ANGELA   Oh I bet that pleased Lol...

(LAURENCE enters in a fury, stripping off his gingham frock and apron and straw hat as he goes. He just drops them on the floor. He pulls off his bright ginger wig and drops that too.)

LAURENCE   It certainly did please Lol! I'm going to strangle that little runt in the interval with a pair of my plastic tits.

(ANGELA opens out the costume and helps LAURENCE into it. It is an atrocious Little Miss Muffet type dress. Then he sits at the make up table and puts on a blonde Marilyn Monroe type wig and re does his make up, talking all the time.)

They get one bloody television appearance and then they think they know it all. Won't even learn a bloody script properly. Too bloody important for that. Too busy signing autographs for pre-pubescent fans outside the stage door. Do you know that, in the last week, he's screwed at least three of those girls hanging around outside? I doubt if any of them are older than fourteen.

GEMMA   You've only got five minutes.

LAURENCE   I know Gemma dear, thank you. Unlike other people, I know what I'm doing.*(GEMMA exits)* That's probably because I don't shove little packets of white powder up my nose like Teen Dream does. Angela, give me the danglers.

(ANGELA opens a jewellery box and hands him some long diamante earrings.)

ANGELA   I know you don't like Jack but I think you might just be displaying a touch of professional jealousy.

LAURENCE   *(spluttering)* Professional jealousy ! Don't you dare use the word "professional" when talking about that little toe rag! That is the trouble my dear. If he was a "professional", he would have served his time in the theatre, he would not forget three pages of dialogue and he would not be strutting about here like some pathetic peacock in heat.

ANGELA   Peacocks don't have a "heat".

LAURENCE   Shut up. I need more lipstick. *(With satisfaction at his reflection)* What an old tart I am!

ANGELA   Yes. What an old tart. Who would think that this was once the man described as Sir Laurence Olivier's successor 'in looks and talent?'

LAURENCE   Angela, don't be a snob. You're very waspish today. I thought we were past the menopause.

ANGELA   Oh be quiet and finish your lipstick.

LAURENCE   Ooh, pardon me I'm sure. *(He stands and looks at himself in the full length mirror)* Right. Back to the fray. Am I OK? Skirt not hooked up in my knickers is it?

ANGELA   You look wonderful. A poem to hideousness.

LAURENCE   You say the nicest things. *(He exits)*

(ANGELA picks up the discarded costumes from the floor and hangs them up)

ANGELA	Past the menopause. Yes I certainly am. Past everything except caring.
	Ah well, time for an anti-depressant. *(ANGELA gets a bottle of pills out of her handbag and downs one with a glass of water. She raises the glass in mock toast to the picture of LAURENCE'S mother)* Here's to all the women in Laurence Bedford's life – the dead and the nearly dead. *(She sits down and sighs)* Well, haven't I cornered the market in self-pity today?
	(HARRY sticks his head round the door)
HARRY	Is the coast clear?
ANGELA	*(jumping)* Oh Harry! You gave me a start! What are you doing here for the matinee? We haven't got to the interval yet.
HARRY	Oh I was just rattling around at home and I thought I'd come and see my best girl. How are you then. *(He kisses her and ANGELA responds awkwardly)* Come on. Give us a proper kiss. I haven't seen you for two days.
ANGELA	Sorry love. I'm just a bit tense today. I hate Christmas Eve shows.
HARRY	I love em. It means a whole day off tomorrow. Just you and me and a real family Christmas.
ANGELA	*(hesitant)* Yes...Harry, about tomorrow...
HARRY	Don't you worry about a thing. I've got it all arranged. The family are putting on a real spread. Christine's a bit worried about you being used to the best food and everything but I told her you weren't like that. I told her you were just like the rest of us.

ANGELA	That's silly.
HARRY	Well you are like the rest of us.
ANGELA	No, I mean that she should be worrying about it. What have you been telling her?
HARRY	Just that you're a lady – the lady that I love – the lady that I'm going to marry.
ANGELA	Harry...
HARRY	And that you used to be a wonderful actress...
ANGELA	*(embarrassed)* Oh Harry!
HARRY	Well you did. I told you. I thought you were wonderful when you were twenty five and you haven't changed.
ANGELA	*(smiling)* I can't picture you as one of my young fans.
HARRY	You don't know the half of it.
ANGELA	I think I do. You must have told me a hundred times that you went to all six performances of Midsummer Night's Dream at the Old Vic.
HARRY	Got me through National Service that experience. Your lovely face and your lovely voice.
ANGELA	*(abruptly)* A long time ago. Before the menopause.
HARRY	Eh?
ANGELA	Never mind. Look you'd better go. Lol will be back in a minute.
HARRY	I just don't understand why we have to keep quiet about everything. Why don't you want him to know? I mean...for Chrissake...
ANGELA	We go back a long way...I'm his best friend...oh I don't

know. I just don't want to hurt him, that's all. He's all alone at the moment...

HARRY He's not your responsibility. I'm your responsibility now. There's a ready-made family waiting for you, if you want it. Just think Ang. Tomorrow we can watch the grandchildren open their presents, we can have a few drinks, Christmas dinner, go for a walk with the dog, watch telly, have a few laughs...come on.

ANGELA *(hastily)* Yes. OK. But you'd better go now.

HARRY *(realising)* You haven't told him about tomorrow, have you? Have you?

ANGELA *(ashamed)* No.

HARRY *(annoyed)* Why!?

ANGELA I just haven't had the right opportunity that's all. Look I promise I'll tell him. I promise. Now go. Please.

HARRY *(being stubborn)* I've a good mind to stay here and tell him myself.

ANGELA *(horrified)* No! Not in the middle of a performance. He's too highly strung!

HARRY *(scornful)* Too highly strung. What does he thinks this is bloody Hamlet?

ANGELA It's just as important to him Harry, you should know that. He's a perfectionist, whatever he does. Now please GO!

HARRY *(reluctantly)* Alright. But come and see me a bit later, eh?

ANGELA I'll try, It depends what needs to be done.

HARRY *(firmly)* Try. *(He kisses her and leaves.)*

(ANGELA looks depressed. She sits down at the mirror and looks at herself.)

ANGELA   Fancy my 'lovely face' getting anyone through National Service. Jesus. Fat chance now lady. *(Looking in the mirror)* Oh look! *(sarcastically)* There's another wrinkle. *(She looks at the portrait again)* Well we can't all afford face lifts can we Gloria? Most of us don't have adoring sons who hand over their money when we snap our fingers. *(quietly)* Some of us don't have sons at all and never will have. Oh God, there I go with the self-pity again. Give it a rest Ang, it's only the Christmas blues.

FADE ON DRESSING ROOM

SPOTLIGHT IN FRONT OF STAGE

(LAURENCE as Dame Trot comes on, carrying a bucket, and leading DAISY the cow on a rope.)

LAURENCE   Hello children. Have you seen my son Jack? No? Ooh he's probably gone up that beanstalk again. Has he? Ooh, I hope he'll take care. I'm very worried about that nasty giant you know. Yes. Jack says he's got great big hands...and great big feet...and great big...don't look so eager missus, you don't know what I was going to say! I was going to say! I was going to say...great big bushy eyebrows! My Jack had to go back up there you know because we've run out of money again. Yes we have. All that gold he stole from the giant it's all gone! I don't know how. I mean I only bought essentials. Yes I did. Let me see, what did I buy? *(he gets a list out of his bosom)* I bought a gold plated toilet seat...ooh, it's lovely and warm when you sit down... everyone should have one...I bought seven fur coats, one for each day of the week... I bought 30 wigs, one for each day of the month do you like this one? This is my Marilyn Monroe special. Lovely isn't it? And I bought three hundred and sixty five pairs of shoes, one for each day of the year. Now you don't think that's too extravagant do you? No of course you don't. We women need our little comforts don't we? Talking of little comforts who's that lovely looking man sitting next to you dear? Yes, you – in the third row. If I had a man like that I wouldn't be wasting my time coming to a pantomime. If she doesn't appreciate you dear, I know someone who will. *(She winks)* But, as I was saying, Jack didn't want to go back up to the giant's castle. Ooh he was cross with me! But I said to him "Mummy's reached that time of life when she needs pampering" that's right isn't it ladies? What do we have sons for, if not to look after us in our old...er...middle age? Right? Ooh and of course I forgot! I went and bought back Daisy the cow. Aah. Say aah boys and girls. Aah.

(DAISY does a little curtsey – SFX)

Yes that's right Daisy, you do a little curtsey. She's so polite you know. Very well brought up. Now Daisy, it's time for you to give some milk.

(DAISY looks at LAURENCE and then shakes her head – SFX)

What do you mean no!? She's sulking you know, because we sold her. Aren't you?

(DAISY nods. LAURENCE gets out a handkerchief from his bosom and his voice breaks.)

Oh Daisy, we were ever so upset about it. Really we were.

Weren't we boys and girls? Yes. Cried buckets we did. *(change of voice)* Talking of buckets Daisy, I'm just going to put this bucket down here and let you give the milk in your own time. Here we are.

(LAURENCE puts the bucket down. DAISY kicks over the bucket and shakes her head at the audience, then does a little dance. Appropriate sound effects and music.)

Ooh you naughty cow! Isn't she naughty? Yes you're very naughty. Now come on. Stop behaving badly and do as you're told.

(LAURENCE picks the bucket up and puts it down again. DAISY kicks over the bucket again. Sound effect of a loud raspberry.)

Ooh! Now she's getting rude! Right! I've had enough of this. Now listen here Daisy. If you don't give me some milk this instant, it's...it's...beefburgers!

(DAISY does a frantic little dance and starts to run round the stage. LAURENCE runs after her, shouting "Stop, come back here!" etc. Chase music. DAISY stops. LAURENCE stops and pants heavily.)

Ooh, I'm getting too old for this! Now look Daisy. This is serious. You have to give me some milk, otherwise I won't have anything to put on poor Jack's cornflakes, will I boys and girls? What's that? Oh she wants to whisper something to me.

(LAURENCE bends down and DAISY whispers in her ear.)

Oh, do you know what boys and girls? I feel so ashamed. Daisy is absolutely right. I didn't say please. Isn't that terrible. You should always say please you know, when you want something, shouldn't you? Yes. Well Daisy. I'm very sorry. Could I please have some milk dear?

(DAISY squats down to sound effect and a bottle of milk appears from her rear end – SFX.)

Ooh Daisy you clever girl! I hope you don't want the empties back because I'm not putting them back up there! Come along now, let's go and see if Jack has come home. Come along. Bye bye boys and girls.

(Exit music)

FADE ON FRONT OF STAGE

LIGHTS ON DRESSING ROOM

> *(Exit music and applause are heard faintly. LAURENCE comes in on a great high.)*

LAURENCE   What applause! That's the best so far.

ANGELA   *(listless)* The Daisy routine went well then did it?

LAURENCE   Brilliant. *(He starts to remove costume and wig and throw them on the floor. ANGELA automatically picks them up)* Pat and Eric were wonderful. I put the bucket down *(He mimes)* Eric kicked it over, Pat gave me the look, the children laughed. I put the bucket down again, Eric kicked it over, Pat made a rude noise and winked Daisy's eye, the children roared. I tell you, it was a masterpiece of comic timing. A symphony of ribald entertainment. Where's the champagne?

ANGELA   *(dismayed)* Oh you're not going to start so early?

LAURENCE   Oh dear. Are we depressed? Tough. It's Christmas Eve and I

	have another show to get through before I go home to my cold and lonely bed and I need a drink.
ANGELA	You have another show and a *half* to get through. You won't make it if you're drunk.
LAURENCE	I've done some of my best work on two bottles of champagne. Stop being such a bore. *(PAT and ERIC come in, they are still wearing their respective halves of Daisy the cow. PAT is carrying the head.)*
PAT	Lol, we were wonderful weren't we?
LAURENCE	Darlings! I was just telling the Queen of Misery here that it was a masterpiece. Come in, come in, have a glass of bubbly.
PAT	*(giggling)* Ooh lovely! Don't mind if we do.
ERIC	Not too much though. Can't be drunk in charge of a cow now can we? *(he laughs)*
LAURENCE	*(imperiously pointing at the fridge)* Angela, please. *(ANGELA goes to the fridge in the corner, which is packed with bottles of champagne and takes one out, reluctantly.)* Glasses please, my sweet. *(ANGELA gets the glasses and hands them round.)* Have one yourself too Angela. Might cheer you up.
PAT	*(sweetly concerned)* Oh, are you down Angie. What's the matter? Tell Auntie Pat about it.
ANGELA	I'm fine.
ERIC	I expect she'll cheer up when a certain stage door keeper arrives.

(ANGELA looks anxiously at LAURENCE who pretends to ignore the implications of it all)

LAURENCE   Not even Madam Angela is desperate enough to take any notice of a mooning old pensioner. *(savagely)* Are you Angela?

ANGELA   *(ignoring him)* How did your audition go the other day Eric?

ERIC   Wonderful. I think we're in with a chance.

PAT   Oh more than that sweetheart. He said that our reputation had preceeded us as one of the best comic animal acts in the country. I think we've cracked it this time.

LAURENCE   So. The starry world of television has finally opened up for you eh? Don't forget darlings. Screw them down to a nice long contract.

ERIC   Oh if we get it, it should take us through several series.

ANGELA   Which animal?

PAT   Well, Eric's doing the kangaroo and I'm doing the koala being the smaller of the two of us.

LAURENCE   And what will it be called?

ERIC   Pro tem it's "Bushtime Ballads".

LAURENCE   Ah. It's Australian.

ANGELA   *(sarcastically)* No, the kangaroo's Chinese and the koala's from Shepherd's Bush.

PAT   *(seriously, not getting the sarcasm)* No it is Australian Ang. But made for the British market.

ERIC   By a Japanese production company.

LAURENCE   *(not really caring)* Fancy.

(There is a brief silence while conversation dries up.)

PAT   Weren't we good today?

LAURENCE   *(beaming)* Breathtaking!

ERIC   The best.

               (GEMMA sticks her head round the door.)

GEMMA   Ang. Can you do a favour for Jack?

LAURENCE   Sorry darling, I think Angela's a bit past it now...

ANGELA   Shut up. What is it?

GEMMA   *(handing over a pair of trousers.)* Split the seam on
               his trousers. Can you do a quick repair?

ANGELA   Sure. *(She goes to get her sewing box)*

LAURENCE   *(pompously)* Officially Gemma, Angela is supposed to be
               my dresser and wardrobe mistress not the whole world's
               and certainly not for scruffy little oiks who shouldn't be in
               the acting profession.

GEMMA   *(very adept at dealing with actors)* Oh Laurence, I know
               that Angela works for you but you don't mind really, do
               you? Pretty please?

LAURENCE   *(grudgingly)* I suppose not. *(Smiling at GEMMA)* How is
               your father? How is Ian? *(To PAT and ERIC)* Did you
               know that Gemma's father and I worked in rep together?

PAT   Yes. I think you told us.

GEMMA   Er...actually...

LAURENCE   *(interrupting)* So how is he? Still in the business? He always
               was a great character actor, old Ian. I thought he was
               absolutely terrific in that TV series about the policeman.

GEMMA   Yes. My dad is still in the business. He's in a play in the West End at the moment. But you were in rep with my *grandad*, Laurence. My dad – Peter – was in the TV series. My grandad's retired now.

LAURENCE   *(disconcerted)* Are you sure? Your *grandad*?

GEMMA   Yes. 'Fraid so.

LAURENCE   *(slightly depressed)* How wonderful to be part of a theatrical dynasty.

GEMMA   *(a bit embarassed)* Fifteen minutes until the balloon scene everyone.

ANGELA   *(smiling at LAURENCE's discomfort)* Want some champagne Gemma?

GEMMA   No thanks. I'd better go and check all the props. *(she exits)*

LAURENCE   Her *granddad*! I can't believe that.

ANGELA   *(rubbing it in)* She's only nineteen. You are nearly seventy. What's not to believe?

LAURENCE   Take no notice of her, it's the Change.

ANGELA   You said earlier that I was post menopausal. You can't have it both ways.

PAT   *(hastily)* Oops, lovers tiff. Time for us to depart young Eric.

ERIC   Certainly is. Time for a wee before I change into Lol's boyfriend.

PAT   *(she giggles)* Be gentle with Eric in the next scene won't you? Thanks for the champers darling *(She gives LAURENCE an exaggerated kiss on the cheek and they exit.)*

ANGELA   *(savagely)* Lovers tiff! What a stupid thing to say!

LAURENCE   You are determined to have a row today aren't you?

ANGELA   No. Don't be silly.

LAURENCE   What is it? *(sweetly)* Haven't we had our oats lately?

ANGELA   *(exasperated)* Oh for God's sake!

LAURENCE   If my memory serves me correctly, you were quite good in bed, in your younger years. That sort of thing is supposed to improve with age.

ANGELA   *(bitterly)* It wasn't good enough for you though was it? I think we had sex twice before you convinced yourself that you were gay.

LAURENCE   *(seriously)* You know that's not true.

ANGELA   *(angry)* I don't know anything of the kind. One minute we were lovers and the next minute you were moving in with Piers. Its hard enough to lose a man to another woman but to lose him to an older man is a level of pain I never want to experience again.

LAURENCE   *(anguished)* Don't. No matter how bad you feel, don't say anything bad about Piers. Not now he's dead.

ANGELA   *(remorseful)* Sorry. I didn't mean it. He was always very kind to me and you were both together for such a long time I suppose it must have been right for you.

LAURENCE   Yes. *(softly)* What's the matter with you today love?

ANGELA   *(close to tears)* Oh I don't know. Christmas I suppose. You know. The whole thing of being alone in a family season. The whole thing of being a woman who's past it thinking about all the things other women have, like husbands, children, grandchildren...

LAURENCE   Grandchildren! Jesus Ang!

ANGELA   *(ratty)* Oh that's it. Be sarcastic. Why change the habits
of a lifetime.

LAURENCE   *(putting his arm around her)* Sorry. Sorry old thing. No. I
don't mean old thing. God Angela, you're a very attractive
woman. Don't let this time of your life get to you. I do
understand. Mother went through the same thing...

ANGELA   *(bitter again)* Oh *Mother.* I wondered when she would
come into it.

LAURENCE   *(trying to help)* Come on Ang. Stop being so angry at the
world. You've got me. *(enthusiastic)* You and I will have
the best, the most elegant Christmas Day ever. Just like
when Piers was alive. Do you remember that year we all
flew to New York on Concorde? Extravagance personified
my darling.

ANGELA   *(quietly)* I remember you crying in the toilet on the way
back.

LAURENCE   *(embarassed)* Don't be silly! Too much booze.

ANGELA   That was when you found out Piers had cancer wasn't it?

LAURENCE   *(quietly)* Yes.

ANGELA   How many Christmases did the three of us spend together?
Nearly thirty. I should have been ashamed of myself. All
those years of being the world's most embarrassing
gooseberry...

LAURENCE   *(defensive)* It wasn't like that! We wanted you there.

ANGELA   *(insisting)* You didn't for the first two years. You know

damn well it wasn't until I took that overdose that you
started making me 'one of the family'...

LAURENCE   *(firmly)* Not true...

ANGELA   And this is what I'm left with. The memory of thirty years
of desperation and pity. That's why I hate Christmas.

LAURENCE   *(briskly)* It will be different this year. It will. Just you and
me. I've got something special planned.

ANGELA   Oh Lol. It won't work. You know it won't. Just the two of

us. No charming and wise Piers chaperoning the wayward
actors as they make fools of themselves with too much
booze. You and I don't have anything to talk about
anymore.

LAURENCE   *(refusing to be miserable)* Ridiculous! I won't continue this
conversation a minute longer. Tomorrow you are going to
be whisked away to paradise! So you'd better put your glad
rags on my girl and your best disposition. *(realising the
time suddenly)* Christ! I'd better get ready!

*(He busies himself dressing and repairing his make up,
while ANGELA sews JACK's trousers very quickly.)*

I hate this next scene. Going up in that bloody hot air
balloon gives me palpitations.

ANGELA   It only goes up six feet.

LAURENCE   Six feet is quite enough for an ageing dame to cope with
thank you very much.

ANGELA   You're getting too old for this...

LAURENCE   *(throwing down his make up in disgust)* Oh my God! Just
because You've got the "Whatever Happened to Baby Jane"

miseries, there's no need to write everyone else off!

ANGELA   *(spiteful)* And you're putting on weight. I have to keep repairing the fake boobs in your frocks because your own boobs are getting so big, they're pulling the frocks apart.

LAURENCE   *(vengeful)* Right, that's it you mean spirited cow...
(His outburst is interrupted by a frantic Jack who rushes in the room)

JACK   Angela, where's the bloody costume?!

ANGELA   *(frantically)* It's here, it's here...

JACK   *(very ratty)* About fucking time woman...

LAURENCE   *(losing it and grabbing JACK'S shirt in fury – mustering his best 'actor's' voice)* Don't you dare to speak to her in that tone of voice, you little shit. That 'woman', that goddess of needlecraft, was an actress of magnitude before you could even pee in a potty...

ANGELA   *(nervously)* Cut it out Lol...

LAURENCE   I'll have you know that MISS ANGELA MARTIN has lain in the arms of Lord Olivier himself. That alone is worthy of deep respect...*(He releases JACK, who staggers back slightly but seems unfazed.)*

ANGELA   *(annoyed)* Lol, stop it...

JACK   *(with some interest)* Get away...really? You and Olivier?

ANGELA   *(sighing)* I was the understudy for Desdemona at the National Theatre during the last Ice Age. He cried all over me on the bed every Thursday afternoon at understudy rehearsals...

LAURENCE   Ah but he meant it. I watched him. The man was never that good an actor.

ANGELA   Shut up Lol.

GEMMA   *(shouting offstage)* Show number coming up! Places
            everybody!

JACK   *(cheekily to Angela)* I bet you've had a few more
            interesting lovers eh? Wanna teach me all you know
            darling?

            (LAURENCE splutters into his glass of champagne.)

ANGELA   *(icily)* No I do *not*. I doubt that you have the brains, or the
            tackle, to appreciate quality sex.

            (LAURENCE laughs)

JACK   *(exiting, annoyed)* Screw you sister!

ANGELA   *(calling after him)* In your dreams!

LAURENCE   *(calling after him)* I'm available dear heart!

ANGELA   *(laughing as well)* I ought to be really cross with you.

LAURENCE   *(very amused)* You handled yourself superbly my darling!
            You have lost none of that acerbic wit for which you were
            famed. Have another glass of bubbly. *(he pours)* What was
            it you said to Richard Burton on the set of "Beckett"? He
            said *(He assumes a Burton growl)* "Can't you put more
            feeling into that line?" And you said *(he raises his voice an
            octave)* "I can, but only if you put *less* into feeling me. My
            ass is black and blue."

            (They both fall about laughing.)

            (being camp) Now give auntie a kiss and send her on her
            way to the death defying balloon stunt.

ANGELA	Go on. Break a leg.
LAURENCE	I sincerely hope not my dear. *(He exits)*
	(ANGELA smiles to herself and sips her champagne. She goes over to the mirror and tries on a pair of outrageous earrings. She is beginning to cheer up. HARRY enters furtively, with two cups of tea.)
HARRY	Has he gone?
ANGELA	*(startled)* Ooh! Yes, Yes he's gone to do the dreaded hot air balloon bit.
HARRY	Oh well, he'll be gone for a while then. Brought you a cup of tea. I thought you were going to come and see me. Been busy have you?
ANGELA	Er, yes...Had to mend a few costumes. Jack's trousers as well.
HARRY	What you got those on for? *(pointing at earrings)*
ANGELA	*(pulling them off)* Oh just a bit of a laugh. Jack, would you believe, propositioned me.
HARRY	Go on. Saucy little beggar. *(thoughtlessly)* Got no respect for age.
ANGELA	*(depressed again)* No.
HARRY	*(spotting the glasses)* Oh. Been drinking champagne I see. Don't suppose you want this cup of tea then?
ANGELA	No. Don't be silly. I wasn't drinking champagne. The others were. No. This cup of tea's just what I wanted.
HARRY	He drinks a lot doesn't he?
ANGELA	Who? Lol? No, not really. He's been a bit depressed since his friend died...that's all.

HARRY   There all the same, these has been actors. Once they're not top of the tree any more, they all hit the bottle.

ANGELA   *(defending LAURENCE)* That's not fair Harry. Lol's not a has been.

HARRY   *(sniggering)* No, more like a never was.

ANGELA   *(enthusiastic)* Oh no! He was wonderful when he was young! He really was. Like a god. When he stood on stage he had the most wonderful face, body and voice. You only get that combination once every decade or so.

HARRY   *(sarcastically)* So why is he where he is now? I mean. Bloody pantomime dame. Not that it's not a skill in itself. I've seen some cracking dames in this theatre – believe me. But I've never known a classical actor do the job - province of your stand up comedians and professional drag queens, that is.

ANGELA   It's a long and complicated story. Mainly to do with *her*. *(ANGELA nods at the picture and pulls a face.)*

HARRY   What his *mother*?

ANGELA   Yes. Gloria. She bled him dry. She couldn't have cared less about his talent, she just wanted him to earn big money so that she could get her hands on it. She pushed him into all sorts of dreadful things private and professional. She was an evil, evil woman.

HARRY   Well he must have been a bit soft to do everything she said.

ANGELA   Mm. I suppose he was really. But you don't know what tactics she used. No one could wheedle, nag, blackmail or apply pressure like she could. She always dangled the carrot and he always tried his damndest to get that carrot, but he never could. Like a donkey pulling a cart.

HARRY   What carrot was that then?

ANGELA   The one thing he always wanted and she didn't have it to
             give. He always wanted her to love him and be proud of
             him and he never, ever realised that she wasn't capable of
             loving anyone except herself.

HARRY   *(unsympathetic)* Silly sod.

ANGELA   Yes he is.

HARRY   *(dismissive)* I haven't got much time for actors. I mean I
             love the theatre and all. Love my job. Admire a really good
             professional job of work, but I haven't got a lot of time for
             a load of sensitive ponces disappearing up their own
             backsides.

ANGELA   *(miffed)* Hang on! I'm an actor – or was!

HARRY   Oh yeah. But you're normal. Anyway, you were an actress
             but you grew up. You wouldn't want to go back to it now,
             would you? *(ANGELA doesn't answer but HARRY doesn't
             notice)* Anyway, what are you doing between shows?

ANGELA   *(defeated)* Nothing. Absolutely nothing.

HARRY   Let's go for a meal down that little Italian place eh?
             I passed it this morning. It's all decorated up, like
             Father Christmas's grotto. Let's have a nice break for
             an hour eh? Just you and me.

ANGELA   *(shrugging)* I don't see why not. Lol will have a nap
             anyway.

HARRY   *(irritated)* Oh who cares what he's doing! I'm talking about
             you and me! Come on Angela. Let's have some time to
             ourselves.

| | We won't get much of it tomorrow, once the family arrive. Mind you, I suppose we might find a bit of time in the morning for a bit of passionate lovemaking, what'd'you reckon, eh? |

ANGELA   *(smiling)* We'll have to see what Father Christmas brings.

(They kiss passionately. HARRY breaks off.)

HARRY   God! Don't get me too lathered up now, otherwise I'll have to have a cold shower! I'm going before I lose control. See you later.

ANGELA   Yeh. See you outside at five o'clock. OK?

HARRY   OK.

(HARRY snatches another quick kiss, then exits.)

ANGELA   *(to herself)* Mrs Angela Brand. Housewife. Step mother and grandmother. *(she sighs)* Is it real? What happened to Angela Martin, RADA Gold Medal winner, the promising actress of her generation? Fizzled out into nothing that's what.

PAT   *(sticking her head round the door)* Cooee? Fancy a bit of company?

ANGELA   Yes. Sure. Come in. Want another glass of champagne?

PAT   Ooh no better not. Got to get changed back into the cow in ten minutes. Wouldn't mind a cup of that tea though.

ANGELA   Oh I didn't make some. Harry just brought this in for me. You can have it if you like. It was sweet of him but I didn't really want it.

PAT   *(taking the tea)* Ooh ta. *(slyly)* Getting serious I think...

ANGELA   Sorry?

PAT	Our stage door keeper. Getting serious about you.
ANGELA	Yes. He wants me to spend Christmas Day with him. *(hastily)* But don't say anything to Lol.
PAT	Oh that's a tricky one Ang. What are you going to do?
ANGELA	I don't know Pat. *(serious)* Tell me. Have you ever wanted to settle down? You know. Suburban home. Kids. Same routine. Forget the theatre?
PAT	Not me darling! Eric and I couldn't live without treading the boards! Would have been nice to have kids though. Just didn't happen. I think that's why we enjoy the job so much. We're playing to kids all the time. If it's not panto, it's summer shows, or kid's parties. We're lucky. We struck the right note when we left rep and started with the animal costumes. Never out of work. Mind you some of the kids nowadays can be little monsters. We're thinking of stopping the kid's parties. We had several costumes ruined last year. Kids trying to stuff ice cream and cake in the camel's mouth. Then there was one little horror who drew pictures all over the teddy bear's backside with felt tip pen. I said to the mother "You shouldn't allow your child to ruin other people's property like that". She just laughed. The wrong people have got too much money nowadays. This family had a bloody great house. Range Rover in the driveway. Couldn't move for the kid's toys. And they were a pack of bloody vandals. Still, if we get the television series then we'll be laughing. Won't have to do the kid's parties anymore. What was the question?
ANGELA	I asked if you ever wanted to settle down. You answered the question.

PAT	Oh...yes. Does Harry want you to settle down with him then?
ANGELA	Yes. He's got all sorts of plans. He thinks that we could both run a theatrical costumiers or something. Get a little shop somewhere and do fancy dress. You know.
PAT	*(quietly concerned)* And do *you* want that, love?
ANGELA	*(confused)* I don't know. Sometimes, when Lol's doing panto I hate it so much, I just want to get away from it all. Then when Lol's doing other stuff straight stuff where he doesn't need me and I do freelance work for film and television, I can't wait to get back to this. *(she indicates the dressing room generally)* I don't know. I'm just so confused at the moment.
PAT	Why don't you go back to acting? You've got the contacts Ang. And you're the right age now to go back.
ANGELA	*(laughing)* What do you mean!?
PAT	Well I was talking to Sheila the other week. You remember, Sheila Harris. She was in last year's panto as the Fairy Godmother.
ANGELA	Oh yes.
PAT	Well she's just got herself a super job in a new tv soap, playing the lead character's mother. She said she's never been in such demand! Honest. She said "Pat, no one wanted me when I was in my forties but now I'm older there's no end of parts on offer." Really she did. And I mean, the way you look. You know...elegant...you could get loads of stuff. I heard that the RSC is doing a tour of Romeo and Juliet next season. Now how about that? Tailor

made for Lady Capulet I should say!

ANGELA   I wouldn't have the confidence any more.

PAT   Rubbish. You been around Lol too long that's your trouble!

ANGELA   What's that got to do with it?

PAT   Well...and I mean this in the nicest possible way... don't get me wrong...but he's a bit overpowering isn't he? Likes you to run around after him. Always putting you down a bit without thinking I expect. I've said to Eric lots of times "He's always putting Ang down. It's not right". Catch me putting up with that from Eric. Mind you I'm lucky with Eric. One of nature's gentlemen.

ANGELA   Yes you are lucky. How long have you been married?

PAT   It's our silver wedding next year. We're thinking of hiring the stage at Wimbledon and having a big do. You'll be invited, of course.

ANGELA   *(envious)* Lovely.

PAT   Yes, we've already designed the cake. A friend of ours is going to make it. It's going to be all the animals that we've played like a big zoo only in cake form.

ANGELA   *(beginning to crumble)* Wonderful. Shouldn't you be getting ready?

PAT   Oh my God. Chatting away nineteen to the dozen! Eric will be waiting for me hooves on chewing at the cud! Here's your mug. *(earnestly)* I hope I've helped Ang. You can talk to me anytime, you know that. Woman to woman. Men just don't understand us do they? *(She exits)*

(GEMMA sticks her head around the door.)

GEMMA | I thought you'd like to know that, despite the hot air balloon wobbling about a lot in mid-air. Laurence did a lot of really good ad-lib jokes and the scene went very well. *(GEMMA disappears)*

ANGELA | *(desperate)* Dear God. I'm living in a farce.

LAURENCE | *(making a flustered entrance)* What's that about a farce?

ANGELA | *(with artificial brightness)* Yes. I've been offered an acting part in a new Feydeau farce that's going to open in the West End. What do you think about that?

LAURENCE | *(cruelly dismissive)* Acting? You? Don't make me laugh.

ANGELA | *(hysterically overacting)* Oh but I will! I shall make everyone laugh with my sparkling and witty portrayal.

LAURENCE | Are you serious?...Is this on the level? *(He looks hard at her. She says nothing)* No you're not. Stop trying to wind me up.

ANGELA | *(aggressive)* Now why would *me* making a statement about returning to acting wind you up? Should it not give you pleasure? Should you not be filled with delight at the prospect of me becoming a creative artiste again?

LAURENCE | *(withering)* Oh give me a break, Hedda Gabler. Why have we reached the "I'm just an unfulfilled woman" stage so early in the day? We usually don't get to that scene until the second half of the second show when you are suffering vodka and tonic withdrawal symptoms.

ANGELA | *(marvelling at him)* Another put down. It's like breathing to you putting me down. Everyone notices it you know. Pat and Eric have noticed it.

LAURENCE | *(sarcastic)* So now we care about the opinion of two sad

old people who spend their life inside a cow costume, do
we? Look Angela, by all means continue with this orgy of
self pity but could you please, in the meantime help me into
my sodding ballgown? *(He starts to undress. ANGELA gets
the ballgown off the rack and helps him into it, while they
carry on their conversation.)*

ANGELA   Of course! Do excuse my self pitying remarks. I do realise
that the only one allowed to spew forth self pity by
the shovelful around here is you.

LAURENCE   Darling I am being remarkably tolerant of you today, only
because the performance is going so well and because I'm
hoping that you are going to get it all out of your
system before our inexpressibly wonderful Christmas Day
happens. *(patronisingly)* It's no good trying to upset me.
Grubby little oiks who forget their lines can't upset me;
unstable hot air balloons can't upset me; and you thrashing
about in your elderly female angst certainly can't upset me.
So just give it a rest, pour me a quick glass of champers and
give us a kiss.

ANGELA   *(With a murderous look on her face, she gets a glass, gives
it to him and pours him a drink. He drinks it down in one
and she waits to deliver her coup de grace.)* I'm not
spending Christmas Day with you.

(There is a silence)

LAURENCE   *(stricken)* What?!

ANGELA   I'm *not* spending Christmas Day with *you* – I'm spending it
with Harry and his family.

LAURENCE   *(doesn't believe her)* Don't be so bloody childish.

ANGELA   I'm not being childish. I'm being mature. I don't want to
               spend Christmas Day getting drunk with a has been actor
               laddie who only wants me along because he can't face being
               alone. I'm going to spend Christmas Day with normal
               people who want my company because they like me.

LAURENCE   *(quietly)* And how long has this been planned?

ANGELA   Quite a while actually. Harry's daughter has made all the
               food. Harry and I have bought the family their presents.
               We're going to watch the grandchildren open them on
               Christmas Day and then we may go to church or for a walk
               or watch telly whatever normal people do.

LAURENCE   *(with a deadly smile)* How charming. How bijou. I should
               like to see you give the acting performance of your life my
               darling. "Angela Martin brought such conviction to her role
               as a normal person that we all went out and bought her a
               subscription to the parish magazine." You stupid cow! Do
               you really think that you can be one of them? *(sensing a
               weak spot)* You haven't actually met them have you? His
               family?

ANGELA   *(uncertain)* No.

LAURENCE   *(savagely)* No. And what do you think they will do? Clasp
               you to their suburban bosom and initiate you into the secret
               rites of being a Tesco's shopper? Or perhaps they will pipe
               you and him into the house on Christmas morning beneath
               an archway of crossed soup ladles.

               *(He grabs her round the neck and forces her to look into
               the make-up mirror.)*
               (savagely) Look at yourself madam! Look at yourself! You

look like a refugee from a bad Ivor Novello production – all gypsy skirts and bangles. You should have "Art Farty" tattooed on your bloody forehead. You're so obviously theatrical I'm surprised you can even get on a bus in the morning without the conductor auditioning for you.

(He lets her go. She starts crying. He is trying to hurt her because he is so frightened.)

You pathetic woman. Do you really think that you can have a life with a man like that?

ANGELA   *(desperate)* Yes. Yes I do. Because I *want* it. Any life is better than this...this...pitiful existence of yours.

LAURENCE   *(domineering)* I don't have time for this now. We'll talk about it in the interval.

ANGELA   *(defiant)* No we won't. I have no interest in discussing my private life with you.

LAURENCE   *(sulkily)* Fine. Piss off then. *(He goes to the door, turns back and says theatrically)* Congratulations Miss Martin. You have succeeded in upsetting me. I am now going to go on stage and kick the shit out of Jack and then I shall come back here and consume a whole bottle of champagne. The second half of the matinee is in great jeopardy now thanks to you.

ANGELA   Do what you like. You're a pathetic excuse for a man.

LAURENCE   How charming.

(LAURENCE leaves. ANGELA wipes her tears and starts hanging up clothes. GEMMA knocks at the door and ANGELA opens it. GEMMA is standing there with a large wicker food hamper in her arms.)

GEMMA   It appears that this food hamper from Fortnum and Masons is for Laurence.

ANGELA   *(clapping her hand to her mouth)* Oh my God! I forgot all about Lol's Christmas Eve beanfeast!

GEMMA   *(puzzled)* Beanfeast?

ANGELA   Yes. One of Lol's little traditions. He orders a hamper of food for the Christmas Eve matinee, then invites the principals into his dressing room for the two intervals. We are supposed to have the savoury stuff and champagne in the matinee interval and the dessert stuff and more champagne in the evening interval.

(Realising that GEMMA is standing in the doorway awkwardly)

Oh, come in, for goodness sake, and put the thing down! It must weigh a ton! Let me help you.

(Between them they struggle in with the hamper and put it on the floor in the centre of the room.)

GEMMA   Well that sounds jolly civilised! Do I get an invitation too?

ANGELA   Of course, darling. *(wickedly)* But you must promise to tell Lol more about your Granddad. He would just adore to catch up.

GEMMA   What about Jack? I know that he and Laurence don't exactly get on. Perhaps I should just keep quiet about it…

ANGELA   *(sensing an opportunity to really upset LAURENCE)* No! Don't be silly! Lol's little Christmas Eve soiree could be just the thing to build a few bridges – don't you think?

GEMMA   *(not convinced)* Well, if you're sure…

ANGELA   Absolutely! Tell Jack Lol would love to have him join us all.

GEMMA   OK. It sounds like fun. *(GEMMA exits.)*

ANGELA   *(to herself, with grim satisfaction)* Oh it's going to be fun, alright. In fact…I can hardly wait to see the look on Lol's face when the party gets started. *(She smiles).*

FADE TO BLACKOUT

END OF ACT 1

UP THE BEANSTALK AGAIN

ACT I SCENE II

The interval in LAURENCE's dressing room. ANGELA has laid out a table with the savoury items in the food hamper – paté, cheeses, crackers, olives, cheese straws etc. There are also paper plates and napkins and 6 champagne glasses. There are a row of wooden chairs set out. LAURENCE enters, pulling off his wig.

LAURENCE	Ah! The goodies have arrived! Splendid!
ANGELA	Yes. I'd forgotten about the Christmas Eve ritual.
LAURENCE	*(taking off his shoes with some relief)* God, that's better! Ritual? You make it sound like it's something unpleasant.
ANGELA	Mm. Well who knows, with one of your little parties? I seem to remember that things haven't always been full of joie de vivre in the past.
LAURENCE	*(irritated)* Jesus, Ang! One party that goes wrong and you bear a grudge forever!
ANGELA	Yes, well. It did happen to be my fiftieth birthday party and, thanks to you, it was an unforgettable experience.
LAURENCE	*(sulkily)* I'd just had too much to drink, that's all…
	(PAT pokes her head around the door.)
PAT	Are you ready for us?
ANGELA	Absolutely. Come in, come in.
	(PAT enters, followed by ERIC, who is clutching a wrapped Christmas present and a bunch of flowers.)

ERIC	*(giving the present to LAURENCE)* Here you are old man – just a little something from Pat and me. Happy Christmas. Oh, and some flowers for the lovely Angela. *(He gives ANGELA the flowers.)*
LAURENCE	How kind darlings!
ANGELA	Oh you shouldn't have! They're lovely!
LAURENCE	I feel a Christmas kiss coming on! *(He leaps up and grabs PAT, bending her over backwards and kissing her in mock passion.)*
ERIC	I say! Steady on, Lol! Don't get her used to that level of passion or she'll be expecting it from me when we get home!
LAURENCE	*(laughing)* Now your turn, Baron! *(He grabs ERIC in the same embrace and kisses his neck noisily. Everyone laughs. At that moment JACK and GEMMA walk in.)*
JACK	Not interrupting anything are we?
	(LAURENCE and ERIC straighten up and look embarrassed.)
ERIC	Just a bit of larking about between the Baron and Dame Trot.
JACK	Yeah, right. I always thought you two fancied each other.
LAURENCE	*(smiling evilly)* No, you're wrong. Its you I've always fancied, dear heart.
JACK	OK. Well I'll pass on the groping if you don't mind.
LAURENCE	*(frostily)* Is there some reason you're here?
ANGELA	*(hastily)* Don't be silly Lol! Jack's invited to the party, of course.

LAURENCE   *(hissing at her)* He's what?!

ANGELA   *(firmly, with a satisfied smile)* That's what you said, Lol
                dear. Invite all the principal actors, you said.

LAURENCE   By what definition does he qualify as an actor?

JACK   Fine. If I'm not wanted…

ANGELA   *(firmly grabbing JACK's arm and propelling him to a chair)*
                Don't be silly! You really must learn to understand
                Laurence's vicious sense of humour. He doesn't mean half
                the things he says.

LAURENCE   *(acidly)* Don't I?

ANGELA   Come on everyone! It's Christmas Eve and we're having a
                little friendly interval party. Let's get in the spirit shall we?
                I'll get the champagne. *(She goes to the fridge and gets out
                two opened bottles, then she starts pouring it into the
                glasses.)*

PAT   *(looking at all the food)* Oh Lol, this all looks very
                scrummy! Is it Fortnum's again?

LAURENCE   But of course. I wouldn't get a hamper from anywhere else.

GEMMA   *(helping herself to some cheese and crackers)* Angela said
                that this is a sort of tradition with you, Laurence.

LAURENCE   Absolutely. For the last…um…twenty years, I think, I have
                always hosted interval parties on Christmas Eve.

GEMMA   Yes, Angela said that you have the savoury stuff in the
                matinee interval and the dessert in the evening matinee.

PAT   *(helping herself to some cheese straws and olives and filling
                up a plate for ERIC as well)* Ooh yes, it's lovely! Eric and I
                really miss Lol's little parties when we're working in

another pantomime.

ERIC   I should say! Remember three years ago in Chester, Pat?

PAT   Oh God, that was miserable! We had to have a completely dry theatre because Melanie Godfrey, who was playing the Fairy Godmother, had just come out of rehab and the management banned alcohol backstage. She was in a foul mood because she was sober and we all crept around on eggshells on Christmas Eve. You could have cut the atmosphere with a knife.

ANGELA   *(looking at LAURENCE pointedly)* Yes, I know what you mean. Bad atmospheres backstage are always a little more tolerable when you have some alcohol around.

LAURENCE   *(sarcastically)* Angela, of course, speaks from personal experience – having downed more bottles of booze than the captain of the Titanic.

(Everyone laughs except ANGELA, who glares at LAURENCE. By now, PAT, ERIC and GEMMA are seated with plates of food. ANGELA and LAURENCE just have glasses of champagne. JACK has nothing.)

GEMMA   *(noticing JACK has nothing)* Can I get you some food, Jack?

JACK   *(smiling at her)* OK babe. Just a few olives and a bit of Edam cheese. Don't want to break my diet. *(GEMMA gets up and fills a plate for JACK)*

LAURENCE   *(almost sneering)* Diet?

JACK   Yeah. Atkins. Gotta keep in shape in front of the camera.

LAURENCE   *(being deliberately difficult)* Why?

JACK	Because the camera makes you look heavier.
LAURENCE	*(acidly)* Really? I wouldn't know, only having been in several long- running TV series.
JACK	Oh yeah? When was that, then? Before colour?
LAURENCE	*(stung)* No, it was not before colour.
JACK	But it hasn't been recently though.
ANGELA	*(deciding to stick her oar in)* Nineteen eighty two wasn't it Lol? Inspector Morse?
LAURENCE	*(sulkily)* You know it was.
GEMMA	Oh yes! That's when you worked with my granddad!
LAURENCE	Was it, Gemma dear? Was it really? Yes! Do you know, I believe you're right! Although we had worked together many times before that, in the theatre - *(addressing this pointedly to JACK)* when we were young actors, learning our craft.
JACK	I suppose you went to drama school?
LAURENCE	Yes I did actually. I went to RADA. I don't imagine you went to a drama school.
JACK	Stage school. I've been acting since I was eight.
LAURENCE	Ah. Stage school. *(dismissively)* Isn't that where they breed little sweeties for telly adverts and soaps?
JACK	*(laughing)* Kind of, I suppose.
GEMMA	Jack's been voted Sexiest soap star for three years running – haven't you Jack?
JACK	Yeah. Whatever.
LAURENCE	Yes. I think I'd worked that out from the screams emitted

by pre-pubescent girls every time he comes on stage.

PAT   Ooh, it must be exhausting being stalked by teenage girls! I've seen you fighting your way through them to get out of the stage door every night!

ERIC   Yes! We always wait until you've gone, Jack, so we can walk out unmolested. Not that anyone would mistake me for you!

            (Everyone laughs)

LAURENCE   Ah, those were the days! I remember having to fight off the stage door admirers myself.

ANGELA   Mm. I don't remember you fighting terribly hard – especially in the latter years when the admiring crowd was mostly young men.

LAURENCE   *(chuckling)* How true.

JACK   So how come you ended up doing drag in panto?

            (There is an awkward silence as everyone looks at LAURENCE.)

LAURENCE   *(refusing to be goaded and smiling benevolently, as if to indulge JACK)* Panto, you know, is a greatly underrated art form. Of course, when I first went into it, it was in its heyday really. That was before it was polluted by the introduction of talentless little oiks from the world of daytime television...

            (ANGELA smiles, anticipating a big argument, but, at that moment, JACK's mobile phone rings.)

JACK   *(raising his hand imperiously to cut off any further conversation)* Yes Mike.

(pause) One point two million? Couldn't they make it one point five? *(pause and JACK frowns)* Well, I don't think it's good enough! *(getting angry)* Tell them to stop pissing me about! You tell them I'm worth one point five otherwise I walk. *(pause)* I don't care, Mike. Either I get one point five or you can find yourself another client. *(He turns off his phone)* Fucking agents!

GEMMA   Is this for the Brad Pitt movie?

JACK   Yeah. Trying to nail me down to one point two mill. Just taking the piss because they think British actors are cheap.

ANGELA   *(astonished)* One point two million dollars?!

JACK   *(scornful)* Pounds, babe! I don't get on a plane for less than three million dollars.

LAURENCE   Good God! For your first Hollywood film?!

JACK   If you go in too cheap, man, then they keep you cheap. That's Hollywood's em o. If you place a high value on yourself, then they will too. *(Gets up)* Anyway, thanks for the food but I've got some calls to make.

                (JACK leaves. Everyone else stares at each other in disbelief.)

GEMMA   *(sort of apologising)* He really is very talented you know.

LAURENCE   *(acidly)* Really? Is that the opinion of the profession, or just his opinion?

GEMMA   He's won quite a few awards.

ANGELA   Sexiest Soap Star?

GEMMA   Oh…no…that one is just a sort of joke really. No, he's won a couple of Baftas and an Olivier. Did you see him in the remake of All Quiet on The Western Front? He was very moving.

LAURENCE   *(bitterly)* I'll take your word for it. What did he win the Olivier for? *(sarcastically)* Surely it wasn't something where he had to learn lines?

GEMMA   He did Hamlet.

(LAURENCE splutters into his champagne.)

LAURENCE   Good God! What he actually played the lead role? Or was he just the skull of Yorick?

GEMMA   *(laughing)* You are mean, Laurence! No, he was actually Hamlet. His whole CV is in the programme, haven't you read it?

ANGELA   Oh, Lol never reads the programmes. He finds them too depressing.

GEMMA   *(genuinely puzzled)* Why?

ANGELA   Because – one - they remind him of how old he is and – two – what a serious actor he used to be.

LAURENCE   Shut up.

GEMMA   *(sensing that the atmosphere is changing)* Well, sorry, I'm going to have to cut and run as well. I've got all the props to sort out for Act two. *(She puts her empty plate on the table and makes for the door.)* Thanks for inviting me. *(She exits.)*

PAT   Three million dollars! Fancy that young lad being worth that sort of money.

LAURENCE   *(muttering)* He hasn't got it yet.

PAT   Sorry?

ANGELA   Lol said "He hasn't got it yet." But I bet he will.

ERIC   The money has got silly nowadays, hasn't it? I blame
              Elizabeth Taylor.

LAURENCE   What?

ERIC   Elizabeth Taylor. She was the first movie star to demand a
              million dollars and get it. Then they all started it.

PAT   I know. And when I read that movies cost an average of
              one hundred and fifty million dollars to make...well...I just
              can't get my head around those sort of figures. You could
              wipe out African poverty overnight with the sort of money
              Hollywood spends on films.

ERIC   It makes our combined salary of one thousand pound a
              week look a bit meagre doesn't it?

LAURENCE   *(startled)* Is that how much you make? One thousand?

ERIC   Between us. Yes.

ANGELA   *(sensing that LAURENCE is shocked)* Time for a top up!
              (she gets up and grabs a bottle and starts refilling glasses)
              Pat, Eric, eat some more food. Lol obviously isn't hungry.

PAT   What about you? I haven't seen you eat anything yet. I feel
              a pig eating while you're not.

ANGELA   I shall eat something in a minute, don't worry.

PAT   Well, if you're sure. *(She takes ERIC's empty plate and her
              own and proceeds to refill them.)* This really is lovely food.
              You are so kind Lol.

LAURENCE   *(slightly distant, as though thinking about something)* My
              pleasure.

ANGELA   And thank you both for the lovely flowers. Lol, you haven't opened Pat and Eric's present.

LAURENCE   What? Oh yes! How thoughtless of me! So sorry. I didn't expect anyone to give me a Christmas present. *(He unwraps it.)* Slippers. *(trying not to sound ungrateful)* Nice comfy slippers.

PAT   Well, you are always complaining to Eric about how much those stage shoes make your feet hurt. We though some nice slippers would be just the ticket for offstage.

LAURENCE   *(looking at the slippers uncertainly)* Just the thing. Yes. Very thoughtful.

PAT   So what are you both going to do on your day off tomorrow?

ANGELA   *(hastily)* Not sure yet. What are you doing?

ERIC   Oh it's always the same for us. Lovely really. We go to Pat's mum's house...

PAT   After we've had a nice lie-in, of course, because we'll have been up 'til three at my sister's Christmas Eve party...

ERIC   ...and we have a big Christmas lunch with all of Pat's family and my dad, who's been going to Pat's mum's house for Christmas ever since my mum died.

PAT   Yes, it's just a lovely family Christmas Day, like always.

            (ANGELA looks very depressed and LAURENCE notices.)

LAURENCE   *(being suddenly bright and cheerful)* Well Angela and I are having Christmas Lunch on The Orient Express!

            (PAT and ERIC make appreciative noises and ANGELA looks surprised.)

ANGELA   Are we?

LAURENCE	Yes!
PAT	Oh, it was supposed to be a surprise, Ang, and we've gone and spoilt it!
ANGELA	That's OK. It doesn't matter. (To LAURENCE) Just as a matter of interest, when were you going to tell me?
LAURENCE	In the break between shows.
ANGELA	I see.
LAURENCE	*(enthusiastically)* It'll be dead glamorous, Ang. The train doesn't actually leave Britain, but it poodles around while everyone has this lavish lunch and receives expensive presents from the organisers. We'll be surrounded by the rich and famous and be waited on hand and foot. Whacha think? Eh?
ANGELA	*(smiling)* Sounds wonderful.
PAT	It does! You two have had some exciting Christmas days haven't you?
LAURENCE	We have, we have. What was the best one, Angie? Paris for the day? Monte Carlo? Rome?
ANGELA	Oh, I don't know. I loved it when we flew to Vienna for Christmas lunch.
	(To PAT and ERIC) It was all snowy and beautifully decorated everywhere. We had lunch in some sort of palace with the Vienna Boys Choir singing as we ate. It was magical.
PAT	Sounds lovely. Really lovely.
LAURENCE	I loved the one where we had a two day break, because Christmas Day fell on a Saturday, so we had Boxing Day off as well, and we went to Istanbul.

It was very exotic and beautifully warm.

ANGELA   *(disagreeing)* No. That wasn't my favourite. It wasn't Christmassy at all and I wasn't too keen on the food.

LAURENCE   Ooh no. I remember that. You threw up all the way home.

ERIC   Ugh! Bad luck old girl!

LAURENCE   Ah! Happy days though – eh, Angie? Happy days.

ANGELA   Indeed.

PAT   'Course, you're so lucky – not having any family ties. You can just slope off to exotic parts without worrying that you're going to upset the family.

ERIC   Yes. Pat's mum would be distraught if we didn't turn up for Christmas lunch.

PAT   Well, she is going to be ninety this coming year. I wouldn't like to miss any Christmasses now, just in case…you know…it could be her last one…God forbid.

ERIC   Even if she wasn't that old, we still wouldn't want to miss our family Christmasses. When you're constantly working, like we are, it's nice to have a family to turn to during the breaks.

            (PAT nudges ERIC for being thoughtless. He realises and tries to backtrack.)

            But…that's just the way we feel…it's not everyone's cup of tea…Most people would give their right arm to have your glamorous lifestyle!

ANGELA   It's alright Eric. Stop digging yourself into a hole.

ERIC   Sorry, Ang. Thoughtless of me.

LAURENCE	*(not understanding)* What's he on about?
ANGELA	Eric's feeling guilty because we – you and I – don't have families to spend Christmas with.
LAURENCE	That's silly! I personally couldn't care less about family Christmasses. Anyway, Angela is my family. Always has been and always will be. *(being jokily melodramatic)* Angela and I shall spend Christmas together until the day we die – and beyond.
ANGELA	Beyond?
LAURENCE	Yes. Eternity. You know. Being together forever.
ANGELA	How intensely depressing.
PAT	*(sensing that they have outstayed their welcome)* Well, we must be going now! Come on Eric! We've got to climb into that cow costume again! It's taking us longer and longer you know. What with my arthritic hip and Eric's back, doing double costumes is beginning to get a bit beyond us.
	(She propels ERIC towards the door.) Thanks again, you two, for the lovely Christmas Eve matinee picnic. I hope we're still invited for the dessert menu?
LAURENCE	Of course, my darlings. Wouldn't dream of tackling the Christmas cake without you…*(LAURENCE holds the smile and bonhomie until PAT and ERIC have left, then he becomes instantly depressed.)* Jesus! What have we come down to?
ANGELA	Don't include me in this travesty.
LAURENCE	*(ignoring her)* I mean, is it too much to expect that I can spend Christmas Eve without being reminded that I am old; have not been on television for years and that I need a pair

of old man's slippers? Not to mention having my nose rubbed in the fact that that no-talent piece of shit, Jack, is worth three million dollars and I am worth, apparently, less than the two halves of a pantomime cow!

ANGELA   Are you?

LAURENCE   *(testily)* I am being paid eight hundred pounds a week and they are being paid one thousand.

ANGELA   But you got paid twelve hundred last year!

LAURENCE   I know.

ANGELA   Why didn't you tell me?

LAURENCE   Because you would have made a fuss.

ANGELA   Damn right I would have made a fuss! Especially when you insist on paying me four hundred a week out of your own money!

LAURENCE   But that's only because the management is too mean to pay for a dresser.

ANGELA   I've told you before that I don't want your charity!

LAURENCE   *(annoyed)* And I've told you before that I need you and I can afford to pay for my own dresser.

ANGELA   Not on eight hundred a week you can't!

LAURENCE   You know that Piers left me a lot of money.

ANGELA   Yes, which won't last long if you are subsidising me and your own career! For God's sake, Laurence, what are you thinking of?! Are we going to get to the stage where you are paying them to give you the part of a pantomime dame? Are you insane?

LAURENCE   *(bitterly)* Apparently, yes.

ANGELA   *(seriously and quietly)* Why are we carrying on with this
             farce?

LAURENCE   *(annoyed)* What farce?

ANGELA   You – being a pantomime dame – and being desperate
             enough to buy my costume services when you don't really
             need them. Why are you doing this? Is it because you enjoy
             being humiliated? Well, if so, then fine – but count me out.
             I have had enough humiliation, thank you. I don't need to
             be an ageing has-been actress and your charity case any
             longer!

             (ANGELA puts her coat on and grabs her handbag.)

LAURENCE   Where are you going?

ANGELA   I'm going out to have dinner with Harry.

LAURENCE   What about the second half?

ANGELA   *(angry)* You only have one costume change. You can
             manage yourself. It will be good practice for you –
             managing without a dresser. Because I'm not doing this
             again next year. This is it. Final. Finito. No more. *(she
             makes for the door)* Oh, and by the way, I meant what I
             said about not spending Christmas day with you. I don't
             care if you offered a day trip to bloody Paraguay – I'm not
             going. I'm spending Christmas Day with Harry and you can
             get stuffed.

             *(ANGELA exits, slamming the door behind her.
             LAURENCE downs his glass of champagne and with a
             scream of anger, hurls the glass at the door.)*

BLACKOUT.

UP THE BEANSTALK AGAIN
ACT II

(As the lights go up, LAURENCE is laying on a couch in his dressing room, trying to have a nap but not succeeding. On the floor beside him is an empty champagne bottle and he is clutching an empty glass. He is dressed in an extravagant frock with a feather boa, but does not have a wig on. His mobile phone rings and he picks it up.)

LAURENCE   *(with false bonhomie)* Manny! How are you? Enjoying the office party I hope, you old scoundrel! *(pause while Manny talks)* It's going well. Really. Best Christmas Eve matinee I've done in a long time. *(another pause)* Oh good. Always aim to please the management. What is next year's pantomime then? *(pause)* I think out of the two, I'd prefer Mother Goose. Yes. Angela did some good costumes for that one. It would be a pity to waste them. And where is that going to be on? *(pause)* Ugh... not too keen on that. I thought you said that the next time would be a London theatre? *(pause. LAURENCE's reaction is a bit hostile)* I'm not that old Manny! What about somewhere like Bromley or Dartford – somewhere close to London? *(Pause. He listens and looks disgusted)* TV stars again! Well the only answer my dear, is to make me into one. *(pause)* No, I'm serious. It's about time I did some TV. Haven't done anything since the eighties. Start me off with a cameo role in one of those hospital or police things and then see if you can get me into a soap. *(irritable)* Stop laughing Manny! I'm serious. In fact I think I should be working up to doing Lear at my age. What about that? If comedians can do

Shakespeare... Be a great sales pitch. Panto Artiste doing
Lear. Give it some thought. Make a great angle on all the
chat shows.*(pause)* Good man. Have a good Christmas.
*(He puts the phone down and is thoughtful for a moment.
Then he fantasises that he is on a well-known chat show
and begins talking to an imaginary interviewer.)*
Yes, well, it's true that I have had a very varied career. I did
several years in rep, learning the business, and then had a
lengthy period at the Old Vic, in it's heyday. *(He pauses,
pretending to listen to a question)* Why didn't I continue as
a classical actor? Well, I was young and other media
beckoned, you know. Richard Burton had the same idea –
so did Peter O'Toole. In fact there was a whole generation
of us who decamped from the theatre into films at that
time. *(He pauses again, pretending to listen to a question)*
No, I didn't stay in films, it's true. But that's because there
was a lot of exciting television at that time. To be honest I
wasn't really into all that Hollywood stuff like Burton. I
like England too much and my mother was alive and
needed me around. She was widowed very early. It was very
sad. She adored my father and really needed some
companionship. But I had a very successful career in
television in the seventies and eighties. *(He pauses for another
question)* How did pantomime come about? Well, it was a
fluke really. Someone asked me if I'd ever considered it.
Actually it was a dear friend of mine who was doing panto
at the time. It looked like great fun, so I gave it a whirl. And
here I am, twenty years later, still putting the frocks on. I
think, you know, that it is the hardest discipline of all, in the
theatre, panto. You need enormous energy and there is a

huge element of interaction with the audience – especially in the parts that I play. Any actor will tell you that comedy is far harder than tragedy and playing to audiences that consist largely of children, is the hardest of all. *(He drops back into reality)* Mainly because the little buggers have the attention span of a gnat! Oh shit, who am I kidding? Have another drink Laurence, why don't you, and then tell them about playing King Lear, for which you are supremely qualified. All that madness- just the ticket. I do it every morning in my bathroom. I rage at the sun for coming up every day – I babble and foam at the mouth at the perfidious nature of so-called friends – I.......

(He hears quiet voices and a low laugh outside the door. He jumps up in a fury and flings open the door to reveal HARRY and ANGELA about to engage in a furtive kiss).

LAURENCE   *(venomous)* Good God! There are two geriatrics coupling outside my dressing room. How disgusting! *(He goes back to the couch.)*

HARRY   *(angry)* I'll lay one on him...

ANGELA   *(firmly)* No Harry. Leave it. He's not worth it.

HARRY   He can't speak to us like that!

ANGELA   Just ignore him. Believe me, that's the one thing he hates above all else being ignored. Now just go and do your work love. I'll deal with this.

HARRY   *(uncertain)* You sure?

ANGELA   Yes. *(She pecks HARRY on the cheek)* Now go on. Off you go. *(She closes the door, takes her coat off, hangs it up and busies herself with tidying up.)* I see we've consumed at least one bottle of champagne then.

Or is it more? No. If you had drunk two you would have left the empty bottle out with the other one for effect.

LAURENCE   O most pernicious woman!

O villain, villain, smiling damned villain...

ANGELA   Oh good. Fine. We're going to retreat behind Shakespeare. See if I care.

(JACK enters)

JACK   *(still seething about the scene before the interval)* You ageing shit! Don't you ever pull that trick on me again....

ANGELA   What did he do?

JACK   *(really angry)* He pulled a load of bollocks during my song. Pulling faces in the background – making the kids laugh and stuff, while I was singing. Put me off my stride. *(To LAURENCE)* I'll crucify you, if you ever try that again, you has-been!

LAURENCE   *(smiling)* Angels and ministers of grace defend us!

Be thou a spirit of health or goblin damn'd,

Bring with thee airs from heaven or blasts from hell

Be thy intents wicked or charitable

Thou com'st in such a questionable shape

That I will speak to thee: I'll call thee Jack

JACK   *(to ANGELA)* What's he on about?

ANGELA   It's Shakespeare dear. Hamlet actually. Laurence is very angry with me and he's doing what he always does when he's very angry with me he spouts Shakespeare.

JACK   *(shaking his head)* He's lost it. But it's a pretty classy way to slag someone off eh?

ANGELA   Actually I think it's very pretentious, and I always have. It's just Lol's way of showing off. He can't summon up his own insults, so he gets Shakespeare to do it for him.

LAURENCE   Let me be cruel, not unnatural
              I will speak daggers to her, but use none.

JACK   *(fascinated by LAURENCE)* How long can he keep spouting like that?

ANGELA   Indefinitely. I gather he's upset you dear?

JACK   Yeah. He pulled a load of bollocks during my song. Put me off my stride. Does he know a lot of Shakespeare?

              (LAURENCE snorts in derision)

ANGELA   His knowledge of the Bard is encyclopaedic. Now if you don't mind I do have things to do...

LAURENCE   *(to JACK as he rises from the couch)* You go not, until I set you up a glass. *(He gets another bottle of champagne out of the fridge and starts to open it.)*

ANGELA   No! No more. You've had enough...

LAURENCE   The potent poison quite o'ercrows my spirit.

JACK   No thanks. I don't do booze.

LAURENCE   *(There is a moment stunned silence while he takes in this information. Then he recovers himself and looks at JACK with some distaste.)*
              A good sherris sack hath a two fold operation in it.
              It ascends me into the brain: dries me there all the foolish and dull and cruddy vapours which environ it; makes it apprehensive, quick, forgetive, full of nimble fiery and delectable shapes; which, deliver'd o'er to the voice, the tongue, which is the birth, becomes excellent wit.

ANGELA   Now we're in trouble. He's moved on to Henry 1V. Lol,
                give me that bottle. *(She tries to get it from him. He
                swerves away and continues his speech. He is in command
                and not at all drunk.)*

LAURENCE   The second property of your excellent sherris is, the
                warming of the blood; which, before cold and settled,
                left the liver white and pale; which *(He almost spits at
                JACK)* is the badge of pusillanimity and cowardice; but the
                sherris warms it and makes it course from the inwards to
                the parts extreme. It illumineth the face, which, as a
                beacon, gives warning to all the rest of this little kingdom,
                man, to arm; and then the vital commoners and inland
                petty spirits muster me all to their captain, the heart, who,
                great and puffed up with this retinue, doth any deed of
                courage; and this valour comes of sherris. So that skill in
                the weapon is nothing without sack, for that sets it a work;
                and learning, a mere hoard of gold kept by a devil till sack
                commences it and sets it in act and use.

JACK   *(smiling)* Amazing. I didn't understand a bloody word.

LAURENCE   *(scornfully)* Peasant!

ANGELA   Yes well, it isn't for your benefit, it's for mine. Now come
                along, out you go.

JACK   But I need my costume mended again!

ANGELA   Here's my sewing kit. Take it to Pat. I haven't got time now.
                Go on. Out. *(She pushes him through the door.)* Well, that
                was a pointless exercise wasn't it. Lol?

LAURENCE   A man cannot make him laugh; but that's no marvel;
                he drinks no wine.

ANGELA	I think it's about time you stopped being childish and just spoke to me normally please.
LAURENCE	Are you not a strumpet?
ANGELA	I said normally, not bloody Othello, NORMALLY!
LAURENCE	What, not a whore?
ANGELA	Oh Jesus.
LAURENCE	It is the cause, it is the cause, my soul Let me not name it to you, you chaste stars It is the cause. *(He comes up behind her and strokes her neck)* Yet I'll not shed her blood, Nor scar that whiter skin of hers than snow, And smooth as monumental alabaster. Yet she must die, else she'll betray more men, Put out the light, and then put out the light.
ANGELA	Oh piss off. *(LAURENCE laughs)* Right. OK. You want to play it this way. You win. Let's purge this choler without letting blood.
LAURENCE	Aha! *(taking up the challenge)* Shall we play the wantons with our woes, And make some pretty match with our shedding tears?
ANGELA	Um...Of comfort no man speak: Let's talk of graves, of worms and epitaphs; Make dust our paper and with rainy eyes Write sorrow on the bosom of the earth. Let's choose executors, and talk of wills.

(changing tack quickly) Let's talk about me and Harry.

LAURENCE   *(sarcastically)* You cannot call it love, for at your age
The hey day in the blood is tame, it's humble
and waits upon the judgement.

ANGELA   Very clever. *(She strikes a pose of hands clasped in prayer)*
My lord, my lord,
I am a simple woman, much too weak
To oppose your cunning. You are meek and humble mouthed
You sign your place and calling, in full seeming,
With meekness and humility; but your heart
is crammed with arrogancy, spleen and pride....

LAURENCE   *(a howl of anguish)* Not Henry Eight! Goddammit woman,
You know I don't know that stupid play! Oh now you've
spoilt it!

(LAURENCE flounces off in a sulk and ANGELA smiles with satisfaction.)

ANGELA   Good. Now talk properly.

(LAURENCE is still sulking)

Fine. Don't talk at all then. That suits me.

GEMMA   *(sticking her head around the door)* Half an hour to go
before the curtain goes up folks.

ANGELA   Thank you. Now talk. Get it off your chest Lol.

LAURENCE   My days are in the yellow leaf,
The flowers and fruits of love all gone...

(In a rage, ANGELA hurls a hairbrush at him and narrowly misses)

ANGELA   NO! Not Byron, not Shelley, not even Oscar Wilde...YOU!
I want to hear YOU talking. Or don't you have a brain of

your own?

LAURENCE   What do you want me to say?

ANGELA   If you want to insult me or be angry with me, I just want
you to do it in your own words.

LAURENCE   *(quietly)* You can't do it. You can't go off with a man
like that.

ANGELA   What? I can't hear you.

LAURENCE   *(shouting)* I said you can't go off with a man like that!

ANGELA   Oh. And why not?

LAURENCE   He's a moron, a nothing, he's ordinary, he's soulless...
do you want me to go on?

ANGELA   You don't even know him. In fact, in all the time we have
been in this theatre I don't think you have spoken three
words to Harry.

LAURENCE   And do you know why? It's because I have this finely
developed instinct that tells me when a person is worth
engaging in conversation or not.

ANGELA   No, you have a finely developed instinct that tells you
whether you are able to impress someone or not. If they
don't express immediate admiration for you, you don't
bother with them.

LAURENCE   Not true. For Chrissake Angela. The man has nothing to
offer you. You deserve better.

ANGELA   Not true. Harry has a lot to offer me – like peace,
contentment, companionship – things that you wouldn't
understand.

LAURENCE   Oh wouldn't I? Don't you think that I long for those
things? Now that Piers is gone, don't you think that I want

some gentle companionship in life? I had hoped that *you* were going to be my companion.

ANGELA   *(irritated)* Don't give me that. You don't want a companion, you want an acolyte. Well, I'm too old and too tired to play the adoring nymph to your Bacchus. Get someone else.

LAURENCE   Alright I will. I'll embark upon a series of one night stands with young boys. Is that what you want?

ANGELA   Ah. I wondered when you would stoop to emotional blackmail.

LAURENCE   I'd stoop to anything dearie – that's how important you are to me.

ANGELA   You sound and look more like your mother every day.

LAURENCE   *(raging)* Don't think you can carry on working with me if you marry that sad old pensioner!

ANGELA   I told you in the interval, I never want to work with you again. Harry and I are going to open a little business.

LAURENCE   *(sarcastic)* Oh? And what might that be? No, let me guess. Something suited to your respective personalities...I know! A taxidermist! You're going to ply your needle stuffing and sewing up dead animals, and he's going to make glass cases for them.

ANGELA   Pathetic.

LAURENCE   No, no! I have it. *(slyly)* You're going to run a fancy dress shop in some little seaside town catering to the amateur theatre brigade and hooray henry birthday parties.
(He looks at her and knows that he's guessed right)
How *lovely*. You'll live off your glory days in the professional theatre and have cosy little chats with all

the fawning amateur actors that end up on your doorstep.
The rest of the time you'll be cleaning wine, beer and
sick off the frocks you've lovingly sewn by hand. Or you'll
be knee deep in bloody sequins and pushy ballet class
mothers. Sounds like a contented existence.

ANGELA   *(uncomfortable with the truth)* And just what do I have
now that's so wonderful eh?

LAURENCE   *(easing in for the kill)* You have our friendship. You have
the knowledge that you were once, and still are, a
professional in the magical world of the theatre. Life is
exciting, always different. *(He starts to speak into her ear as
though trying to hypnotise her)* You never know where the
business or the audiences are going to take you. You give
joy to people. You entertain them. Every time I go out there
in one of your creations I make people laugh. They
remember me but they also remember the frocks. Everyone
of these outrageous costumes is a product of your
wonderful, rich, fertile imagination. You're every bit an
artiste as I am. Don't throw all that away on people who
don't care. If he loved you, if he really knew you, he would
know that you are too precious to be shut away in a... in a
joke shop.

*(He pauses to let her digest his speech. Then he adopts a
casual tone)*

You know, what you were saying earlier, about going back
to acting. I think that's a good idea. I do, really. I think you
could be wonderful now. I spoke to Manny just now. He's
going to get me some TV work and some straight theatre. I
could speak to Manny about you, he could take you back
on his books. We could get some tours together. They're

casting Romeo and Juliet soon.

ANGELA   I heard.

LAURENCE   Well, there you are. You and me. Lord and Lady Capulet,
                eh? Small beginnings. But I'd give it a go if you would.

ANGELA   *(softening)* You would?

LAURENCE   *(getting over-confident)* Of course. Angela. Don't throw
                what we have away. You know that you don't really love
                him. I know that I haven't been kind to you over the years
                but now that Piers has gone I'm beginning to realise that
                deep down, it's you that I really love...and always have.

                *(There is a moment where ANGELA'S breath is taken away
                by this statement. She has waited a lifetime to hear these
                words. LAURENCE goes to kiss her gently and her face
                twists in pain as she realises that it was just another ploy.)*

ANGELA   *(hissing)* You cruel lying bastard.

LAURENCE   *(admitting defeat with a shrug)* Alright I lied...I think
                I lied...I don't know. I just know that I can't imagine life
                without you...

ANGELA   *(bitter)* No you can't can you? Who else would you get to
                listen to your endless stream of self pity? Who else would
                you get to be your accomplice in this...this act of
                degradation? Who else would be so stupid as to be your
                whipping boy, your little sister, your best friend, your
                adoring disciple...even your sodding substitute mother!

LAURENCE   Don't...

ANGELA   Oh yes. Let's bring mummy into this shall we?

LAURENCE   Oh no Angela. *(trying to be offhand)* Not the old cliché

about "my mother made me a homosexual – if I give her
the wool will she knit me one". Please!

ANGELA   No. I don't imagine that mummy made you into a
homosexual. I don't know, I haven't got a clue. But she sure
as hell made you into a failure. Precious mummy who
suckled you at her withered breast like Lady Macbeth,
while she was murdering your life with her insatiable need
for money.

LAURENCE   *(now he's uncomfortable with the truth)* Shut up. It's not
true.

ANGELA   Dear mummy wants new dresses, so little Lol has to give up
being a promising actor and earn more money doing crap
films. Dear mummy needs money to play at the casino so
little Lol has to do adverts. Dear mummy wants a face lift
so little Lol has to put on some tits and do pantomime.

LAURENCE   *(anguished)* DON'T!

ANGELA   And what about Piers eh? Nice rich Piers. Mummy wants
lots of money to last her into her old age so little Lol is sold
into white slavery to a man old enough to be his father!

LAURENCE   *(he lashes out at her, knocking her over)* You bitch! You
bitch! I told you not to say bad things about Piers.
You…you…empty shell of a woman! You don't know what
real love is…you think your pathetic fumblings with a
succession of men mean something. You were always
jealous of what I had with Piers…you aren't good enough
to clean his shoes – you slut!

ANGELA   *(shaken and bruised)* I do know what real love is. I had it
once, or thought I had it – remember? *(quieter)* You know,

you should feel right at home in this panto. It's like the story of your life. Every time mummy wanted more money, up the beanstalk you would go, to face yet another hideous giant. *(turning to him)* Except now, mummy's gone and you don't have to go up that beanstalk anymore. *(trying to persuade him)* You could even chop it down, if you had the guts.

(LAURENCE stands beneath the portrait of his mother and, in his tear stained make up, he looks eerily like the picture above his head.)

GEMMA   *(Offstage)* Curtain in five!

LAURENCE   *(shakily. Sitting down in front of the mirror and putting on a wig)* I have to go. Oh dear, I look like a disaster. I can't do this anymore...... *(He starts to cry quietly)*

ANGELA   *(realising she's gone too far)* Lol, I'm sorry, I'm so sorry. It's OK. Don't worry. It's OK. *(She starts to repair his makeup for him)*

LAURENCE   *(burying his head in her stomach)* Don't leave me Ang. Please don't leave me. I wasn't lying. I can't live without you.

ANGELA   It's OK. It's OK. Come on Lol. You've got to pull yourself together. There. now, come on. *(She straightens his wig and dabs his eyes)*. Come on. Off you go.

(He stands up mechanically, takes a deep breath and goes out. ANGELA locks the door behind him and breaks down into uncontrollable sobbing. There is a knock on the door which stops her.)

HARRY   *(outside the door, worried)* Angie? Angie is that you crying? Let me in Angie.

ANGELA	Oh Harry. No I'm OK Harry. Just leave me alone for a bit please.
HARRY	Angie, I heard the shouting. If he's laid a finger on you... Please let me in Angie. I'm worried about you.
ANGELA	*(firmly)* Harry,I'm fine. Really I am. Stop making a fuss. I just need to be alone for a while. I just need people to leave me alone.
HARRY	Did he hit you?
ANGELA	NO! Harry PLEASE! Not now! Let me rest for a bit. Please Harry.
HARRY	*(uncertain)* OK. If that's what you want. Are you sure?
ANGELA	Yes. Let me be. Just for a while. *(There is silence. ANGELA talks to herself.)* Let me be. I was living in a farce, now I'm living in a tragedy. What do I do? Have a drink. No, that's what Lol would do. Oh bugger it. I need a drink. *(She helps herself to a drink. There is another tap on the door.)* *(crossly)* Harry please go away!
PAT	*(timidly)* It's Pat, love. Can I help?
ANGELA	Oh Pat. What do you want?
PAT	Look...don't be cross. Harry was worried about you. Said there'd been a bust up with Lol and you wouldn't tell him what happened. He thought you might talk to me. You know... girls together.
ANGELA	*(she goes wearily over to the door and unlocks it)* Are you alone, or is Harry hanging on your coat tails?
PAT	*(opening the door gingerly)* I'm all alone...Guide's honour.
ANGELA	Want a drink?

PAT	I'll keep you company darling, if that's what you want. Was it awful? The row with Lol?
ANGELA	Gut wrenchingly awful.
PAT	Was it about you and Harry? You know...being together?
ANGELA	Yes. Lol, it would appear, is insanely jealous *(she laughs)*.
PAT	But I thought Lol...well I know...he...
ANGELA	Prefers men?
PAT	Yes.
ANGELA	He does. But that doesn't stop him being possessive about me.
PAT	Oh.
ANGELA	I don't know what it is. No, that's stupid. I do know what it is. It's because Lol knows that I'm the only person who has ever truly loved him. Loved him passionately. Cried into my pillow because I love him. Would lay down my life because I love him. In short, Lol would never find another human being, man or woman, who loves him as deeply as I do. And he doesn't want to lose it.
PAT	Oh. I knew you were very good friends...you know...been together a long time and all...but I didn't realise you felt that way about him. What about Harry?
ANGELA	Oh Harry was just an escape. Just like all the others in my life. I just can't love anyone in the way that I love Lol.
PAT	You poor thing.
ANGELA	Don't feel sorry for me. It's of my own making. I suppose I could have really tried. Do you know I once had a relationship with another man that lasted two whole years!

Yes. We even lived together.

PAT   Well how did Lol feel about that?

ANGELA   Ah well, things were different then. Lol had his boyfriend and dear old mum was still alive. He didn't begrudge old Angela having a bit on the side then. I expect he probably knew, I expect he always knew, that no one was ever going to be as good as him in my eyes. But now, I'm showing just a bit too much desperation I suppose. It's frightening him. He knows that I regard Harry as my last chance for a proper relationship and he knows that if I go with Harry, we'll never see each other again.

PAT   Perhaps that would be best...to make a clean break from Lol. I mean you can't go on for ever like this can you?

ANGELA   (miserably) No. But I don't think that I can go away with Harry either.

PAT   Oh Angela, that's a shame. He's such a nice chap.

ANGELA   Yes. Yes he is. And it is a shame. But I know that I would only make him miserable. Lol was right. I can't fit into life in suburbia. I can't fit into Harry's life and his family's life.

PAT   Well you don't know...you might.

ANGELA   It's not something you can try out. It has to be all or nothing. If I said yes to Harry and then walked out on him six months later, it would not only ruin his life but it would ruin his children's life and their families...Oh I can't take that responsibility. I've known for a long time that it wouldn't work. Every time Harry started making plans, I would start feeling claustrophobic. Every time he wanted me to meet his family I would make excuses.

PAT   I don't know what to say love...

ANGELA   There isn't anything you can say. It's just all one big mess.

FADE

LIGHTS TO FRONT OF STAGE

               *(ERIC comes on dressed as Baron Soft Touch leading
               LAURENCE as Dame Trot by the hand)*

ERIC   Here we are my love. I've waited for this chance to get you
               away from the ball and on your own.

LAURENCE   *(playfully tapping him with his fan)* Oh you naughty Baron
               you! *(throwing himself into ERIC's arms and nearly
               knocking him over)* Be gentle with me!

ERIC   Dame Trot...

LAURENCE   Please, call me Euphemia.

ERIC   Euphemia?

LAURENCE   Yes. It's a lovely name isn't it?

ERIC   Yes. Euphemia...I can stand it no longer. Being near you is
               driving me insane!

LAURENCE   *(sniffing his armpits)* Oh dear. Don't tell me my deodorant
               isn't working again. *(to the audience)* I buy Super Strength
               you know. Mind you...once I got it wrong and bought
               Super Glue! Glued my arms to my side. Couldn't put my
               make up on for a week! Silly me!

ERIC   Euphemia, my darling. I mean that I want you to marry me!

LAURENCE   *(feigning shock and faintness)* Marry you! Oh my goodness!
               What a surprise! *(hastily)* Yes.

ERIC   Yes? Oh my happiness is complete, my darling. *(He kisses*

LAURENCE's hand and then his arm and then goes to kiss his lips.)

LAURENCE   *(growling in a man's voice)* Watch it sonny!

ERIC   We'll have a quiet wedding. Just you and me, the vicar, your son Jack and my daughter Alice.

LAURENCE   Oh no we won't!

ERIC   We won't?

LAURENCE   No. I'm going to have the most splendid wedding in the country. I want a wedding dress that looks like a dream. I want sixteen bridesmaids...

ERIC   Sixteen?

LAURENCE   Yes and twelve page boys. I want a golden carriage drawn by eight white horses and I want a fountain of champagne at the wedding reception.

ERIC   Of course, you know, I want you to be happy my darling but who's going to pay for all this?

LAURENCE   Oh that's no problem. *(Calling offstage)* Jack! Jack! Come here mummy wants you!

(JACK appears, wearing an embroidered coast and gold silk breeches..)

JACK   *(acting the happy-go-lucky fellow. He never talks to the other cast members – only out to the audience with a big smile on his face. He knows they are his fans.)* What is it mother? Alice and I were just going to do the waltz.

DAME   Oh doesn't he look lovely boys and girls? My son. He's so handsome. Well dear, I'm afraid you haven't got time for dancing now. Mummy needs you to go up the beanstalk again and get some more money. You see mummy and the nice Baron are going to get married and you wouldn't want mummy to have anything but the best at her wedding would you darling?

JACK   Getting married! That's wonderful mum! Of course you must have a beautiful wedding! I'll change my clothes and go up the beanstalk straight away.

ERIC   But what about the wicked giant?

JACK   I'm not afraid of him! I'd do anything for my old mum. She knows that.

LAURENCE   *(He has suddenly seen the parallel between the plot of the pantomime and his own life. he begins to struggle with his emotions and lose the script.)* I...don't..no you can't...it's wrong...don't...

            (There is an awkward silence. ERIC looks terrified. JACK begins to smirk.)

ERIC   But...but what about the wicked giant?

LAURENCE   *(confused)* Shouldn't have to...go...it's wrong...

JACK   *(almost gleefully)* Gosh mother! You seem tired. Has the Baron been chasing you round the bushes again?

ERIC   Er..don't be silly Jack...

JACK   Come on Baron. You can help me tell Alice that I'm going up the beanstalk again. *(He drags ERIC offstage. ERIC tries to protest but can't get out of it. LAURENCE is left alone, bewildered.)*

PROMPT   I feel awful...

DAME   *(mechanically, still not together mentally)* I feel awful

                        ...*(silence)*

PROMPT	Sending Jack up the beanstalk...
DAME	*(recovering suddenly but weakly)* Yes,yes. I feel awful boys and girls, sending Jack up the beanstalk like that. I shouldn't have done it. My poor boy facing that awful giant. And I've been so naughty spending all the money like that. It doesn't really matter about having a lavish wedding. I must try and stop him. Jack! Jack! *(Exit)*

FADE

LIGHTS ON THE DRESSING ROOM

                  (PAT and ANGELA are still talking)

ANGELA	Don't worry. I know. I just have to sort this out in my own way. I'll have a talk with Harry later.
PAT	You won't do anything silly will you?
ANGELA	*(smiling)* Good God no! Don't worry. I'll pull through.
	(ERIC rushes in, in a state.)
ERIC	Angela! Lol took a prompt!
ANGELA	*(appalled)* Oh my God!
PAT	*(distressed)* Oh no!
ERIC	*(beside himself)* It was a disaster. I couldn't help him. I felt terrible. He just wandered off the script and I lost him. He confused me so much and Jack dragged me offstage. There was this terrible silence and then the prompt. It just seemed to echo all round the auditorium. I thought Lol was going to be sick and then he rallied and carried on.
ANGELA	*(urgently)* You'd better make yourselves scarce both of you. He'll be off in a minute.

PAT	Will he be alright?
ANGELA	No. He hasn't taken a prompt in thirty years. He'll be devastated.
ERIC	I feel terrible...I just couldn't help him.
ANGELA	It's OK Eric. Just go. Quick. Quick.

(They exit and ANGELA stands waiting in the middle of the room. The door opens and LAURENCE comes in and looks at her.)

LAURENCE	*(with total horror in his voice)* I took a prompt.
ANGELA	I know.
LAURENCE	I took a prompt! *(He crumples and starts crying.)*
ANGELA	*(putting her arms around him)* It doesn't matter Lol. It really doesn't.
LAURENCE	It does. I stood there and I couldn't remember anything. for the first time in my life I was frightened really frightened. I could see Eric's face. He looked frightened too. And I could hear my heart pounding. I wanted to be sick. And then I saw Jack's face. There was just a hint of a smirk...just...something malicious...a joy in seeing me down...and I felt hot...rage...I don't know. The words came back and I went on again. I was shaking...I still am....... *(frightened)*Angela!

(He stands rigid, shaking uncontrollably. ANGELA holds him firmly and slowly eases him into a chair.)

ANGELA	*(trying to calm him)* It's alright. Everything's alright. Stop this now. Come on stop this. I'm going to get you a hot cup of tea and some biscuits and you're going to calm down.

(She leaves him and opens the door. PAT, ERIC, JACK and GEMMA are huddled outside, plainly trying to eavesdrop.)

(abruptly) He's OK. There's nothing to see here. Gemma, make yourself useful and get Lol some tea and biscuits. Quickly.

(GEMMA darts off)

JACK   *(smiling)* I bet...

ANGELA   *(grabs him quickly and hisses)* You keep your stupid little mouth shut or I'll bounce you down the bloody corridor!

ERIC   *(pulling JACK away)* Come on you. Have some respect for your betters.

JACK   *(calling back as he is dragged away)* He's not my better, he's just a clapped out old geezer in a frock...

ERIC   SHUT IT!

PAT   Can I do anything, Ang?

ANGELA   No thanks love. All under control. Have you got my sewing kit?

PAT   *(producing it from her dressing gown pocket)* Here.

ANGELA   Thanks. It's OK Pat, really.

                (GEMMA comes back with the tea and biscuits on a tray)

                Thanks. *(ANGELA closes the door.)* Here we are. Hot sweet tea. Now drink it up. Come on. It's good for shock.

LAURENCE   *(quietly)* It wasn't a shock. It was a revelation.

ANGELA   A what?

LAURENCE   A clapped out old geezer in a frock...

ANGELA   Oh that. For God's sake don't take any notice of a poxy teenager who's only been in the profession for five minutes!

LAURENCE   Huh. The Emperor's New Clothes.

ANGELA   Lol, you're wandering. Pull yourself together. You're doing Jack and the Beanstalk.

LAURENCE   *(giving her a withering look)* I know that. I'm not wandering. I am citing the example of the Emperor's New Clothes.

ANGELA   Oh.

LAURENCE   Everyone around the Emperor was too scared to tell him that he wasn't wearing any clothes because they had been told that only intelligent people could see the clothes. It was left to the children to tell him that he was stark naked.

ANGELA   Yes I know the story, what's the point?

LAURENCE   Oh face it. You and Pat and Eric...and me...all the same age all hanging on to our careers in the theatre by the skin of our teeth. If we admit that one of us is past it it's as good as admitting that we're all past it. Don't you see? Only the young fool, with his life in front of him, can point the finger and not be touched himself. *(accusingly)* Why didn't you... you of all people...tell me that I wasn't any good any more.

ANGELA   Oh Lol. What a load of rubbish. You take one prompt. One lousy prompt after you've had a very upsetting day and consumed two bottles of champagne, and suddenly it's the end of your career!

LAURENCE   But you don't understand. In that minute...that terrible minute... that I stood, frozen to the spot, unable to remember one single word, I suddenly saw myself as I really am. It was like I was in the audience looking up at myself and thinking "Jesus, that silly old man in a silly frock and make up. He's past it. He can't remember his lines. He looks ridiculous. He isn't funny. He's just sad." I can't really explain it to you. Unless you've experienced it, it's difficult to understand.

ANGELA   I have experienced it.

LAURENCE   So why didn't you tell me?

ANGELA   *(annoyed)* Not about you! God, even in your misery you're self obsessed! I mean I experienced it about *me...me.*

LAURENCE   When?

ANGELA   The last time I stood on a stage as an actress.

LAURENCE   When you played the mother in The Reluctant Debutante.

ANGELA   Yes. When I played the mother. I was thirty five years old. I couldn't audition for ingenue roles anymore and I didn't feel old enough to play mothers of teenagers but the director obviously thought I looked old enough. I just didn't feel comfortable in it at all and, during one of the scenes where I didn't have much to say, I suddenly saw myself...a very clear picture of myself in my mind's eye...standing on the stage... looking awkward, badly dressed, badly made up, wearing an ill fitting wig. I saw the whole picture. I saw the production itself for what it was third rate a compromise a collection of ill assorted actors either on their way up or on their way down, all selected because they were cheap, not because they were talented. I lost it - there and then - lost the ability to pretend. Just lost it. Couldn't get it back. And that's why I never went on stage again.

LAURENCE   You never said.

ANGELA   Oh it's a terrible admission to make. I felt that I couldn't tell other actors because they would shun me. You know... this profession is built on a gossamer fine bridge between reality and fantasy. Actors have to believe, really believe, in their power to make an audience walk over that delicate bridge into fantasy land, otherwise it doesn't work. The whole thing doesn't work. If I had told any working actor who still possessed that belief in himself, that I had lost it, I might have affected them in some way. It's like that line from Peter Pan "Every time a child says 'I don't believe in fairies', somewhere a fairy dies." I couldn't take the responsibility.

LAURENCE   And now I've reached that point myself. I've lost belief in myself.

ANGELA   *(firmly)* No. You've just woken up to the true horror of what you're doing to yourself, that's all. There's nothing wrong with your abilities as an actor. You still have the power to suspend disbelief in an audience. You just haven't operated on that level for such a long time. I've been telling you that for years. Being a pantomime dame is not for you. This isn't your art form. This has just been your way of punishing yourself and a means of avoiding the truth. You didn't want to do any parts that would involve you in dragging up some real emotions out of your soul, so you took refuge in slapstick. You haven't lost your abilities... your real abilities. You could still do it if you want to.

LAURENCE   No I can't.

ANGELA   *(in mock pantomime style)* Oh Yes You Can!

LAURENCE   *(smiling)* I suppose I can. But not without you. *(She looks irritated)* No listen Angie. I mean it this time. I do really mean it. I'm not spinning you a line, I'm not blackmailing you, I'm not, for once, being selfish. *(being truthful)* Well I am being selfish, I don't know how to be anything else...but what I'm saying is...God's unvarnished truth...I cannot go back to straight theatre without your help and support. No one else knows me like you do. No one loves, or has loved me, like you do. No one. Now, if you really love this... Harry...and you think you can be happy...you go. I'm not going to make any more fuss. I promise. This will be my last pantomime. I'm sure about that. But I won't try to go back to being legit unless you're there.

ANGELA   *(scornful)* Oh I see.

LAURENCE   *(desperate)* No, no, I don't mean it that way! I'm sorry, it didn't come out right. What I mean is, I don't have to go back to the theatre. You know that I don't need the money. I can retire. That's OK. I'll be alright. I was just saying that I would never attempt to make a *comeback* without you there with me. I don't have the courage. You believe in me, have always believed in me, more than I have believed in myself. I couldn't manage it on my own. But that's OK. Retirement would be good. I have the place in France. A bit of sun. Write my memoirs. You know.

GEMMA   *(knocking on the door)* I hope you're OK because you're on again in a minute!

LAURENCE   *(panic)* Shit! Quick! get me into the swimming costume!

    (ANGELA and LAURENCE struggle frantically to get him out of his dress and into an Edwardian Bathing Belle piece.

LAURENCE keeps babbling while they do the change.)

Actually I think I might sell the place in France. Never liked it much really. Piers chose it. More his style really. You know-effete Dordogne. I'm more your rustic Spanish myself. Spain would be good. Always liked Barcelona. That quirky cathedral. I could live there quite easily. Hat! Hat! Where's the hat?!

(ANGELA grabs a large mob cap and sticks it on his head.)

Right. Ready.

ANGELA   *(being supportive)* Knock 'em dead Laurence.

LAURENCE   *(convincing himself that he's fine)* I'm OK now. I feel much better than I have in years. Give me a hug.

(They hug each other tightly. Then LAURENCE gives ANGELA a light kiss on the lips.)

See you in a minute.

ANGELA   Sure.

(LAURENCE exits the dressing room and reappears at the front of the stage. The stage goes dark except for two spotlights. One on LAURENCE in one part of the stage and one on ANGELA, who is seated beneath the picture of LAURENCE's mother. They both speak out to the audience. As each one speaks, the other becomes still.)

LAURENCE   *(Although he delivers his lines with certainty, there is an air of fragility about him, as though he is walking a fine line between confidence and mental collapse.)*
Oh hello boys and girls. Do you like my costume? Do you? It's my swimming costume you know. Yes. The Baron has

invited me up to the castle for a swim. At least I think it's for a swim. He said to me "Euphemia!", that's my name you know, Euphemia, isn't it lovely? Yes. Oh of course you know that, silly me. He said "Euphemia! Come up to the castle and wet your whistle!" That's what he said. So I thought I'd better put my swimsuit on! *(He raises his leg and there is a sound effect of a sliding whistle)*

ANGELA   *(sadly)* I'm sorry Harry, I can't spend Christmas with you and your family and I can't spend the rest of my life with you. I know I've hurt you and I know it's hard for you to understand but I have to stay with Laurence. I've been waiting a long time for him to finally realise that he needed me as much as I needed him.

LAURENCE   I've been a naughty girl, boys and girls...yes I have,really. *(getting out a frilly hanky and pretending to cry)* I've been a wicked, wicked mummy to my son Jack. Do you know, I've spent all the money again that he stole from that wicked giant. I have. Isn't that awful? *(He blows his nose loudly and the hanky has a big hole in it)* I spent it all on dresses and hats and shoes and bags and jewellery...I'm a very selfish woman.

ANGELA   I know. I understand what you're saying. He won't ever be interested in me as a woman, he might go back on all his promises and not give up pantomime. There is always the risk that he might find another boyfriend who will take him away from me, but this is the first time, since we've known each other that we will be really alone together. We might actually find some sort of contentment with each other. Anyway, I'm willing to risk even a few years of having Laurence to myself. It's what I've always wanted. As for pantomime...well...I'm pretty sure that I've made my last frock for Lol.

LAURENCE   The worst of it is that I've sent my poor Jack up the beanstalk again to face that horrible giant. Well I don't like being poor, I really don't. There's another ball at SoftTouch castle next week and I haven't got a thing to wear! Oh aren't I a naughty greedy mummy. boys and girls? Well, I'll tell you, I feel so bad about it that I'm never, ever going to do it again. When my Jack comes down, I'm going to give him a big kiss and say I'm sorry. After he's given me the gold of course. *(He starts to lose control, quietly)* I'm going to say I'm sorry...and...I'm going to say...I love you Jack... you're my son...and I love you more than anything in the world...I will...I'll finally say that... I just...want him to love me for what I am....I just want her to say she's proud of me...that's all I've ever wanted.....*(He starts to cry softly.)*

ANGELA   Please forgive me Harry.

BLACKOUT.

FURNITURE LIST

ACT I SCENE I Make-up table and lighted mirror; a small sofa; a fridge filled with champagne bottles; a dress rack containing all the Dame costumes as per script; large photo or painting of LAURENCE's mother in evening dress; two wooden chairs.

ACT I SCENE II An addition of a small table covered with food (See PROPERTY LIST), two extra wooden chairs; a wicker hamper under the table.

ACT II   The items listed above under ACT I SCENE II should be removed for this Act.

PROPERTY LIST

ACT I SCENE I

To start:	On make-up table: make-up; wigs on wig stands (as per script); jewellery in box; glass of water; hairbrush; fan.
On dress rack:	costumes for Dame (as per script); ANGELA's raincoat and handbag.
On wall:	Christmas cards and a few decorations; Portrait/photo (large) of LAURENCE's mother in evening dress.
In fridge:	lots and lots of champagne bottles.

On top of fridge: tray with champagne glasses.

Page 1:	ANGELA : sewing box with needles and thread.
Page 2:	LAURENCE : change of costumes and wig as per script.
Page 4:	ANGELA: gets pills from her handbag, glass of water from make-up table.
Page 7:	LAURENCE: brings on a bucket, has handkerchief down front of dress.
	PAT/ERIC as DAISY the cow; bottle of milk inside costume.
Page 11:	ANGELA: takes champagne from fridge and 4 glasses.
Page 13:	GEMMA: enters with a pair of trousers in her hand.
Page 17:	LAURENCE: change of costumes and wigs as per script.
Page 18:	JACK exits with a pair of trousers.
Page 20:	HARRY enters with two cups of tea.
Page 23:	HARRY exits with one cup of tea.
Page 28:	LAURENCE: costumes/wig changes as per script.

Page 28:	ANGELA: gets a glass and pours champagne for LAURENCE.
Page 30:	GEMMA: appears with wicker food hamper.

ACT I SCENE II

To start:	Table: laid out with food – paté; cheeses; crackers; olives; cheese straws etc. Paper plates; napkins, knives; forks; 6 champagne glasses.
Page 33:	ERIC enters with a Christmas present and a bunch of flowers.
Page 34:	JACK has a mobile phone in his hand.
	ANGELA gets two bottles of champagne from the fridge.
Page 42:	LAURENCE unwraps present to reveal slippers.
Page 47:	ANGELA exits with coat and handbag.
	LAURENCE throws glass at door.

ACT II

To start:	Extra chairs and table of food have been removed. Flowers Are in a vase on top of the fridge. Empty bottle of champagne by LAURENCE; mobile phone by LAURENCE; costume change by LAURENCE has taken place.
Page 50:	ANGELA enters with coat and handbag and hangs them up.
Page 53:	ANGELA: gives sewing box to JACK and he exits with it.
Page 55:	ANGELA: throws hairbrush at LAURENCE.
Page 61:	LAURENCE: puts on wig and picks up fan.
Page 62:	ANGELA: gets glass and pours herself some champagne.
Page 65:	LAURENCE: enters with a fan.
Page 70:	GEMMA: appears with a tray of tea and biscuits.
Page 75:	LAURENCE: costume/wig change as per script.

LIGHTING AND EFFECTS PLOT

ACT I SCENE I

Start of play: *Music. LIGHTS up on dressing room scene.*

Page 7:   CUE: ANGELA: "Give it a rest Ang. It's only the Christmas blues."

LIGHTS: *down on dressing room.*

LIGHTS: *up on panto area.*

SFX: *jolly entrance music.*

Page 8:   CUE: LAURENCE: "…say aah, boys and girls. Aah."

SFX: *Daisy the cow curtsies (musical sound.)*

CUE: LAURENCE: "Now Daisy, it's time for you to give some milk."

SFX: *Daisy shakes her head. (rattle sound)*

CUE: LAURENCE: "She's sulking, you know, because we sold her. Aren't you?"

SFX: *Daisy nods her head (drum beats)*

Page 9:   CUE: LAURENCE: "…you give milk in your own time. Here we are."

SFX: *Daisy kicks over bucket and shakes her head (rattle sound) and does a little dance (a few bars of jolly music).*

CUE: LAURENCE: "Stop behaving badly and do as you're told."

SFX: *Daisy kicks over bucket (loud raspberry sound).*

CUE: LAURENCE: "…it's…it's beefburgers!"

SFX : *Chase music.*

CUE: LAURENCE: "Could I please have some milk, dear?"

Page 10:   SFX: *Daisy produces a bottle from rear end (sliding whistle sound).*

CUE: LAURENCE: "Bye, bye, boys and girls."

SFX : *exit music – same as p.00.*

LIGHTS: *down on panto area.*

LIGHTS: *up on dressing room.*

SFX: faint applause is heard.

Page 32:   CUE: ANGELA: "I can hardly wait to see the look on Lol's face when the party gets started."

LIGHTS: *FADE TO BLACKOUT.*

SFX: *Music until set dressing for Scene II is complete.*

ACT I SCENE II

To start: *LIGHTS up on dressing room.*

Page 38:   CUE: LAURENCE: "…the introduction of talentless little oiks from the world of daytime television…"

SFX: *JACK's mobile phone rings.*

Page 47:   CUE: LAURENCE: He downs a glass of champagne and with a scream of anger, hurls the glass at the door.

LIGHTS: *BLACKOUT.*

SFX: *Interval Music.*

LIGHTS: *House lights.*

ACT II

To start:	LIGHTS: *up on dressing room.*
	SFX: *Pause until agreed point – then LAURENCE's mobile phone rings.*
Page 65:	CUE: ANGELA: "It's just all one big mess."
	LIGHTS: *down on dressing room.*
	up on panto area.
Page 68:	CUE: LAURENCE: "I must try and stop him. Jack! Jack!"
	LIGHTS: *down on panto area.*
	up on dressing room.
Page 75:	CUE: LAURENCE: "See you in a minute."
	LIGHTS: *Tight spot (but full body) on ANGELA.*
	Tight spot (but full body) on LAURENCE.
Page 76:	CUE: LAURENCE: "So I thought I'd better put my swimsuit on!"
	SFX: *sliding whistle as he raises his leg.*
Page 77:	CUE: ANGELA: "Please forgive me, Harry."
	LIGHTS: *Both spots to BLACKOUT.*
	SFX: *MUSIC.*
	CURTAIN CALLS.